EASY
MEDITERRANEAN

Sue Quinn

MURDOCH BOOKS

Contents

The Mediterranean diet   6

Starting the day   10
Yoghurt & cheese   28-29

Plates to share   38
Olive oil   48-49

Salads & soups   66
Nuts   80-81

Meat, poultry & fish   94
Seafood   110–111

Pasta, beans, rice & grains   122
Grains & pulses   134–135

Vegetables   146
Leafy greens   156–157

Sweet things   174
Fruit   186–187

Index   204

The Mediterranean diet

The traditional Mediterranean way of eating, long praised for its health benefits, is commonly described as a 'diet' but this is a term I loathe. To me, 'diet' has connotations of feeling hungry, strict eating regimes and – most hateful of all – calorie counting. None of these has anything to do with the Mediterranean diet and they don't carry any truck with me anymore (although there was a time when they did). The truth is, the so-called Mediterranean diet is a collection of wonderful and delicious eating patterns followed by people in the region, and it is now widely recognised as the healthiest approach to food in the world.

Eating Mediterranean-style does involve filling your shopping basket with certain foods, to be sure: yoghurt and cheese, olive oil, fruit, leafy greens, nuts, seafood, whole grains and pulses are cornerstones of the Mediterranean kitchen. Ideally, it involves falling into a rhythm with the seasons and eating the freshest produce possible, when it's at its very best. Red meat is eaten now and then, and sugar is reserved for special occasions. But the Mediterranean diet is as much a lifestyle as an eating pattern because it also involves being active and enjoying food, both cooking it and sharing meals with friends and family.

If you're looking for a diet book that contains a prescriptive programme of foods to eat and avoid in order to lose weight or achieve some other specific health aim, this volume isn't for you. If you want to embrace the healthy eating habits of the Mediterranean and enjoy the physical benefits, delicious food and wonderful flavours and ingredients of the region, welcome.

A BIT OF HISTORY

The Mediterranean diet as a healthy eating model, so to speak, is usually traced back to the work of American scientist Ancel Keys[1]. In 1952, impressed by previous studies showing low rates of heart disease on the Greek island of Crete, he set out to explore why Mediterranean eating patterns were so healthy. For 25 years he investigated the diet, lifestyle and heart disease rates of middle-aged men from seven countries, the results of which were published in his famous Seven Countries Study.

The findings might appear unremarkable today, but at the time they were pioneering. Keys found that blood cholesterol, blood pressure, diabetes and smoking were risk factors for heart disease. He concluded that the traditional diets of Mediterranean people in the 1950s and '60s protected them from premature death from heart disease and other illnesses. He identified that these diets were mostly plant-based and contained only small amounts of animal foods. Olive oil was the principal fat, alcohol was consumed in moderation and lifestyles involved plenty of physical activity.

Over the intervening years, a vast amount of research has been done to build on Keys' work. In 2013, UNESCO[2] added the Mediterranean diet of Greece, Italy, Spain, Morocco, Portugal, Croatia and Cyprus to the list of cultural treasures (or Representative List of the Intangible Cultural Heritage of Humanity).

THE HEALTH BENEFITS

For decades, the traditional Mediterranean diet has been praised for being the healthiest in the world and evidence continues to mount that it can help reduce the risk of conditions as varied as heart disease, stroke, diabetes, dementia and even infertility. The mountain of research has reached Everest proportions and covers a wide variety of health problems, but some of the key benefits are in the following areas.

Heart health – numerous studies link a Mediterranean diet to reduced risk of heart disease. A 2013 study[3] of almost 7500 men and women at risk of heart disease found that a Mediterranean diet supplemented with olive oil or nuts reduced the risk of heart disease and stroke by 30 per cent.

Type 2 diabetes – a 2014 review[4] of available research found the risk of developing type 2 diabetes was reduced by 23 per cent by sticking to a Mediterranean diet.

Dementia – numerous studies suggest that a Mediterranean diet can reduce the risk of dementia. A 2015 review[5] of available research found that it was a 'potential strategy' in reducing cognitive decline among the elderly.

Chronic disease – a 2003 study[6] looked at the diets of more than 22 000 people in Greece over four years. It found that the closer people followed a traditional Mediterranean diet, the less likely they were to die from either heart disease or cancer. Overall, people following the Mediterranean diet most closely were 25 per cent less likely to die during the study period than those who were not.

THE MEDITERRANEAN DIET AT A GLANCE

Food habits vary from country to country in the Mediterranean, of course, which makes it difficult to ascribe one diet to the entire region. However, there are many foods and eating habits common to Mediterranean countries and a number of studies have been done to identify the most health-giving features of them all[7]. The Mediterranean Diet Foundation (MDF) revised its guidelines in 2011 after pulling together the latest research. The MDF reconfirmed that plant-based meals sit at the heart of the Mediterranean diet, and it set out recommended intakes of core foods. Importantly, there are factors other than food that contribute to the diet's healthiness, including a relaxed attitude to eating and plenty of sunshine and physical activity. The following is a good guide to what it means to follow a Mediterranean-style diet, based on the MDF's recommendations. But remember: this is only a guide to shape your eating habits, it's not a prescription.

- **Extra virgin olive oil** – with every meal
- **Vegetables** – at least 2 serves every meal, including a range of colours and textures
- **Fruit** – 1 to 2 serves every meal, including a range of colours and textures
- **Cereals** (preferably wholegrain) including bread, pasta, couscous and others – 1 to 2 serves every meal
- **Olives, nuts and seeds** – 1 to 2 serves every day
- **Dairy** – 2 serves every day
- **Wine** – 1 glass for women and 2 glasses for men every day, with meals
- **Eggs** – between 2 and 4 serves per week
- **Legumes** – at least 2 serves per week
- **Fish/seafood** – at least 2 serves per week
- **White meat** – 2 serves per week
- **Red meat** – no more than 2 serves per week
- **Processed meat** – no more than 1 serve per week
- **Desserts** – no more than 2 serves per week
- **Seasonality** – seasonal, fresh and unprocessed food whenever possible
- **An active lifestyle** – at least 30 minutes of physical activity per day
- **Socialising** – cooking, sitting around the table and sharing food with family and friends as often as possible, ideally in the sunshine

KEY INGREDIENTS

The available research suggests that no particular food or food group in the Mediterranean diet is responsible for its significant health benefits[8]. More likely, a combination of all the elements is what makes it healthy. That said, scientists have identified some of the main beneficial components of key Mediterranean ingredients.

Olive oil

Olive oil is a type of mono-unsaturated fat that is now known to lower 'bad' LDL cholesterol levels in the body, as well as raise 'good' HDL cholesterol. Because high HDL cholesterol levels are linked to decreased risk of heart disease and high LDL cholesterol levels are associated with increased risk, olive oil is widely praised as being excellent for heart health. But olive oil is healthy for other reasons, too. It is rich in polyphenols, antioxidants believed to reduce the risk of cancer by easing inflammation and cell proliferation, although as yet there is no solid evidence to support this. Extra virgin olive oil (obtained from the first pressing of olives) is also rich in oleic acid, a mono-unsaturated fat that is believed to have health-giving properties[9]. In addition, there appears to be some evidence that extra virgin olive oil has more health benefits than olive oil.

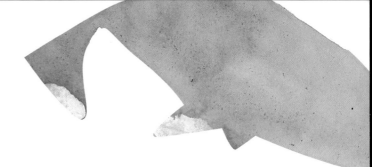

Fruit and vegetables

Eaten in generous quantities, fruit and vegetables have a profoundly positive effect on human health, decreasing the risk of a range of chronic diseases. Researchers believe that the plant-based nature of the Mediterranean diet is one of the key reasons why it is so healthy. The abundant fibre, vitamins, minerals and phytonutrients found in vegetables in particular are known to lower blood pressure, reduce the risk of heart disease and stroke, protect against some kinds of cancer, and lower the risk of eye and digestive problems[10]. Green leafy vegetables, cruciferous vegetables like broccoli and cabbage, and citrus fruit all make key contributions, according to the research. Tomatoes, so abundant in the Mediterranean diet, also have some special properties. When cooked, they are particularly rich in lycopene, an antioxidant believed to reduce the risk of heart attack and cancer[11].

Oily fish

Oily fish are a rich source of omega-3 fats, which are especially good for heart health because of their anti-inflammatory properties and ability to keep blood flowing smoothly[12]. Some studies suggest that omega-3s are even more beneficial to those who have already suffered a heart attack, and that fish oil can keep the heart pumping in a regular rhythm. It is also claimed to help protect against some kinds of cancer and dementia, although clinical studies have yet to confirm this. However, there is some evidence that eating oily fish, such as mackerel, sardines and salmon, two or more times a week can protect against vision problems and rheumatoid arthritis, and control type 2 diabetes.

Wine

Consumed in moderation by healthy people (one glass per day for women and two glasses for men) with meals, wine is believed to have many health benefits, including decreased risk of heart disease, stroke, type 2 diabetes and early death[13]. Red wine in particular contains a wide range of phytonutrients including flavonoid polyphenols (which contribute to its colour) that are believed to heal the body and prevent degenerative diseases such as cancer. But the benefits of drinking wine are quite controversial. Research suggests that some people at higher risk of alcohol-related problems or cancer might want to think twice about a daily glass of wine or two, and drinking more than the recommended amount has health risks including heart disease and stroke.

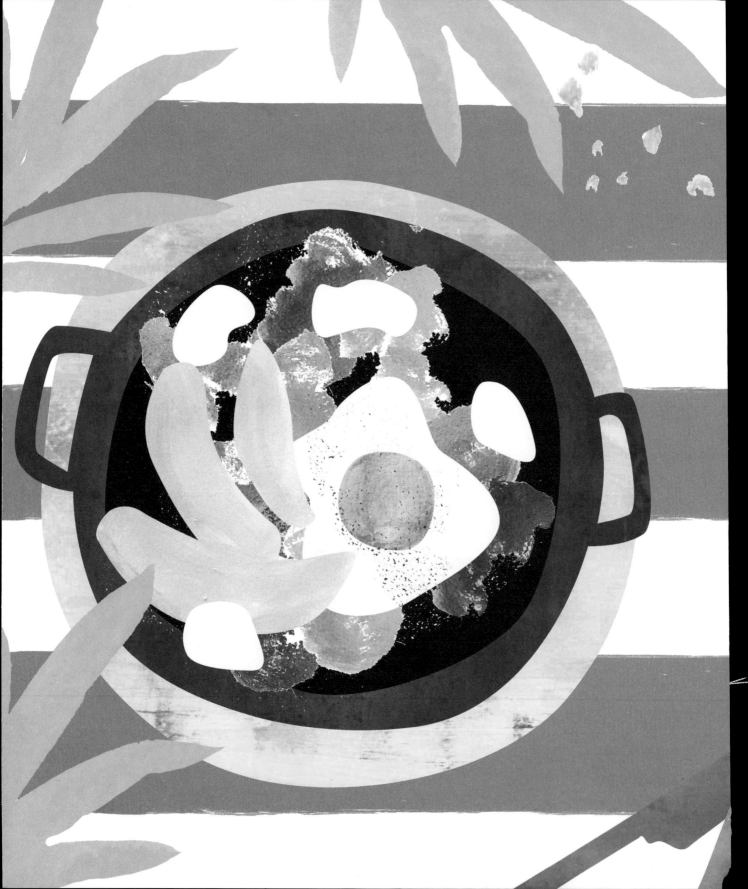

Starting the day

A traditional Mediterranean breakfast is often very basic – nothing more than a plate of cheese, fresh fruit, olives and bread. This gorgeous breakfast bowl stays true to that simplicity, but the honeyed syrup makes it special; even the most conscientious eaters sometimes need a little encouragement to gobble more fruit. Don't be deterred by the cucumber – it's a great way to enjoy this stalwart Mediterranean favourite.

Fruit and cucumber salad with mint and rosewater syrup

Serves 4 generously

200 g (7 oz) honeydew melon
200 g (7 oz) rockmelon
150 g (5½ oz) watermelon
½ cucumber
125 g (4½ oz/1 cup) raspberries
150 g (5½ oz/1 cup)
    strawberries, hulled and
    halved if large
toasted flaked almonds,
    to serve
Greek-style yoghurt, to serve
    (optional)

For the syrup
260 g (9¼ oz/¾ cup)
    floral honey
juice of 2 lemons
1 large handful finely chopped
    mint leaves, plus extra
    for sprinkling
2 teaspoons rosewater

Start with the syrup. Whisk together the honey, lemon juice and chopped mint. Gradually add the rosewater, tasting as you go (the strength of rosewater varies wildly and you're looking for a back note of rose, not a mouthful of perfume). Put to one side.

Use a melon baller to scoop out balls of each melon and place in a large shallow bowl. Peel and halve the cucumber lengthways, then scoop out the seeds with a teaspoon. Slice the flesh into half moons and add it to the bowl with the fruit. Pop the raspberries and strawberries into the bowl, too.

Pour the syrup over the salad, gently tossing as you pour, until everything is coated. Set aside for at least 1 hour to allow the flavours to mingle.

Scatter with the almonds just before serving, add a spoonful of Greek-style yoghurt, if you fancy, and top with extra chopped mint.

I live in the UK where strawberries are cherished as a particularly British fruit, but of course they're not. The most flavourful, aromatic and deep crimson strawberries I've eaten were those I devoured in Greece, Italy and Spain, where they grow in abundance. Sadly, the specimens I pop in my shopping basket at home sometimes need a little coaxing to reveal their full flavour. Roasting is a fantastic way to do this, and the balsamic produces an addictive sweet–sharp sauce. You could easily serve this for dessert, but it's also a lovely way to start the day.

Whipped ricotta pots with roast balsamic strawberries and pistachios

Makes 4 small pots or bowls

2 tablespoons honey, or
   to taste
2 tablespoons balsamic vinegar
a pinch of sea salt flakes
freshly ground black pepper
250 g (9 oz/1⅔ cups)
   strawberries, hulled and
   halved if large
500 g (1 lb 2 oz) ricotta cheese
1–2 pinches of ground
   cinnamon
1 handful pistachio nuts,
   chopped

Preheat the oven to 180°C (350°F).

Whisk together 1 tablespoon of the honey, the balsamic vinegar, sea salt and a little black pepper. Pop the strawberries into a small ovenproof dish that fits them snugly and toss with the honey and vinegar mixture. Roast for about 40 minutes or until your kitchen smells like strawberries and the fruit is tender but still hold its shape – much will depend on the size of your berries. Set aside to cool completely (transfer the berries and every last drop of syrup to a bowl to make this quicker, if you like).

While the strawberries are roasting, whip the ricotta with the cinnamon and the remaining honey (add more to taste, if you like) until light and fluffy, then chill until needed.

To serve, simply spoon the whipped ricotta into bowls, spoon the strawberries and their lovely syrup over the top and sprinkle with the chopped pistachios. If you are in the mood, layer the ricotta, strawberries and pistachios in glasses or jars, finishing with strawberries and a sprinkle of nuts and some sunflower seeds, if you like.

Pancakes evoke weekends and holidays for me, when there's time to potter in the kitchen and then enjoy a long breakfast, ideally outside with the newspapers. I love adding grated fruit to pancake batter. Peaches are wonderful, but apples and pears also work well, as do mushed up bananas. If your fruit is really delicious and juicy, don't feel the need to fry the fruit to go with the pancakes – just serve it sliced, with the sweet juices poured over.

Peachy spelt pancakes with goat's curd and almonds

Serves 4 generously

125 g (4½ oz) spelt flour or wholemeal plain flour (whole-wheat all-purpose flour)
½ teaspoon baking powder
½ teaspoon ground cinnamon
a pinch of salt
1 egg
150 ml (5 fl oz) milk, plus extra if needed
2 teaspoons olive oil, plus extra for frying
6 ripe peaches
3 tablespoons honey
3 tablespoons goat's curd
1 handful toasted flaked almonds

Preheat the oven to 130°C (250°F) to keep the pancakes warm as you cook them.

In a mixing bowl, whisk together the flour, baking powder, cinnamon and salt. In another bowl, whisk together the egg, milk and 1 teaspoon of the olive oil. Gradually stir the wet ingredients into the dry to make a thick batter, adding more milk if needed. Using the largest holes of a box grater, grate two of the peaches into the batter and discard the skins – you will produce a fragrant peach purée. Stir to combine.

Heat a little olive oil in a frying pan over medium–high heat and wipe out any excess with paper towel. Scoop a couple of dessertspoonfuls of batter into the pan for each pancake to make a 10 cm (4 inch) round. Cook the pancakes in batches until golden underneath and starting to bubble on top. Flip and cook for about 30 seconds more. Transfer to the oven to keep warm as you go.

Halve and stone the remaining four peaches, and cut each half into three wedges. Set a chargrill pan over medium–high heat. Warm the honey and the remaining 1 teaspoon of olive oil in a small saucepan. Brush the cut sides of the peaches with the warmed honey mixture, then cook until charred with stripes on both sides.

To serve, top the pancakes with some of the chargrilled peaches, a spoonful of goat's curd, a drizzle of the warmed honey and some flaked almonds.

Not everyone can be bothered to make bread but this really is easy and absurdly satisfying. I warn you that this loaf is also very addictive: it's loaded with flavour, very soft and perfect for dunking in good olive oil or making sandwiches when fresh. If you want to make a simpler loaf, leave out the onion and olive mixture and add 50 g (1¾ oz) mixed seeds with the flours and salt.

Olive oil bread

Makes 1 large loaf

For the dough
2 teaspoons instant dried yeast
330 ml (11¼ fl oz/1⅓ cups) warm water
30 g (1 oz) honey
350 g (12 oz/2⅓ cups) strong flour
100 g (3½ oz/⅔ cup) wholemeal plain flour (whole-wheat all-purpose flour), plus extra for sprinkling
50 g (1¾ oz/¼ cup) fine semolina
1 teaspoon fine salt
2 tablespoons extra virgin olive oil, plus extra for oiling

For the onion and olive mixture
2 tablespoons olive oil
1 onion, chopped
a pinch of sea salt flakes
1 teaspoon herbes de Provence
60 g (2¼ oz/⅓ cup) pitted kalamata olives, chopped

First, start on the dough. Combine the yeast, warm water and honey in a bowl and set aside for 5 minutes or until it starts to froth.

Whisk together the flours, semolina and salt in an electric mixer with a dough hook attachment or in a mixing bowl. Gradually stir in the yeast mixture with a wooden spoon, followed by the olive oil – you should end up with a shaggy, sticky dough. If using an electric mixer, mix for 10 minutes and then tip out onto an oiled work surface and knead for a few minutes more. If working by hand, tip the dough out onto an oiled work surface and knead for at least 15 minutes or until elastic but still quite sticky. Place in an oiled bowl, tightly cover with plastic wrap and set aside somewhere warm for 1½ hours or until doubled in size.

Meanwhile, prepare the onion and olive mixture. Heat the oil in a frying pan and gently fry the onion with the sea salt and herbes de Provence for 15 minutes or until soft and golden. Set aside to cool.

Press your fist into the dough to release the air, then gradually knead in the olives and the onion mixture. Tip onto a lightly oiled work surface and gently flatten into a square. Stretch the top third of the dough out and fold it over towards the middle, then stretch and fold the bottom edge to overlap. Do the same with the left and right sides. Turn the dough over so it sits, seam side down, on the work surface. Using cupped hands, and keeping them in contact with the dough all the time, turn the dough anti-clockwise to form a taut, smooth ball. Place on an oiled baking tray, seam side down. Loosely cover with oiled plastic wrap and set aside somewhere warm until doubled in size, about 1 hour. Or, place the dough in the fridge overnight and return it to room temperature before baking.

Preheat the oven to 220°C (425°F). Cut a couple of slashes in the top of the loaf with a sharp knife, sprinkle the top with wholemeal flour and bake for 30–35 minutes or until the loaf is brown and sounds hollow when you tap it.

The pittas you find in the supermarket are not a patch on these soft, cloud-like versions, and although a little effort to make, they're a pleasure to watch as they puff up in the oven. I put these to loads of uses: wrap them around fillings or use them to make Flatbreads with zucchini blossoms and ricotta (page 52), or I toast them to toss in a salad when they've gone a bit stale. I also love them warm, smothered in butter and Vegemite – not very Mediterranean, I know!

Pillowy pitta bread

Makes 8 pittas

2 teaspoons instant dried yeast
250 ml (9 fl oz/1 cup) warm water
250 g (9 oz/1⅔ cups) strong flour
250 g (9 oz/1⅔ cups) plain (all-purpose) flour or wholemeal plain flour (whole-wheat all-purpose flour), plus extra for rolling
2 teaspoons fine sea salt
100 g (3½ oz) Greek-style yoghurt
30 ml (1 fl oz) olive oil, plus extra for oiling

Combine the yeast and warm water in a bowl and set aside for 5 minutes or until it starts to froth.

Whisk together the flours and the salt in an electric mixer with a dough hook attachment or in a mixing bowl. Gradually stir in the yeast mixture, yoghurt and olive oil with a wooden spoon. If using an electric mixer, mix for 10 minutes and then tip the dough out onto an oiled work surface and knead for a few minutes more. If working by hand, work the mixture into a shaggy dough, then tip out onto an oiled work surface and knead for at least 15 minutes or until elastic but still quite sticky. If you are using wholemeal flour you might need to add a splash of water.

Divide the dough into eight equal pieces and roll into balls. Cover with a clean, damp tea towel and set aside for 30 minutes – the balls should plump up and rise a little.

About 20 minutes before you are ready to bake the pittas, preheat the oven to 220°C (425°F) and place a baking tray lined with baking paper inside.

On a floured work surface, lightly roll out half the dough balls into discs 3 mm (⅛ inch) thick, keeping the unused balls under the tea towel so they don't dry out.

Put the discs on the hot baking tray and bake for 4 minutes – they should puff up in a most satisfying way, but they can have a mind of their own so don't worry if they don't all do this. As soon as you take the pittas out of the oven, wrap them in a clean tea towel while they are still warm – this will keep them soft – and repeat with the rest of the dough balls.

My husband was worried at first that freekeh's robust flavour would be a bit much for porridge, but after tasting it, I had to tear him away from the pan. It's delicious. The rolled oats, dates and nuts mellow freekeh's strong, earthy flavour to make a tasty, filling breakfast. I think marmalade is the perfect accompaniment (my husband says it's a bit like marmalade on toast in bowl form), but jam or honey is lovely, too. I've given quantities for one generous serving here, so scale up the recipe according to the number of mouths you're feeding.

Freekeh porridge with almonds and dates

Serves 1 generously

40 g (1½ oz) freekeh
2 tablespoons rolled oats
250 ml (9 fl oz/1 cup) warm
   milk
¼ teaspoon ground cinnamon
1 small handful toasted
   almonds, chopped
3 medjool dates, chopped
a splodge of honey
Greek-style yoghurt, to serve
marmalade, jam or honey,
   to serve

Put the freekeh and oats in a dry saucepan and stir over medium heat until the grains start to smell mildly toasted. Add half of the warm milk, stirring constantly, then gradually add the remaining milk, stirring constantly.

Mix in the cinnamon, almonds and dates, then gradually add about 200 ml (7 fl oz) water, stirring frequently until the oats are soft and the freekeh is tender but retains some bite – this will take around 15 minutes. You might not need all the water, but then again you might need more, depending on how thick you like your porridge.

Add honey according to taste. Serve immediately, topped with yoghurt and marmalade, jam or honey.

Figs have a natural affinity with salty ingredients – prosciutto is the classic pairing – especially when they're very ripe and sweet. If your figs are a little unripe or hard, brush the cut sides with oil and chargrill them until tender. Whipping the feta with the yoghurt just blurs the cheese's harsh salty edge and makes it very pleasing to spread. If you can't find lavender honey, that's a pity, but any lovely honey will be fine.

Figs, creamed feta and lavender honey on toast

Serves 4

200 g (7 oz) feta cheese
100 g (3½ oz) Greek-style
   yoghurt
4 large slices sourdough,
   country-style bread or
   Olive oil bread (page 19)
olive oil, for brushing
6–8 ripe figs, halved
lavender honey or other floral
   honey, for drizzling

Put the feta and yoghurt in a food processor and blitz until smooth and creamy. Scrape into a bowl, cover with plastic wrap and chill while you get on with the rest of your breakfast.

Heat a chargrill pan until very hot – or use the barbecue if that works for you – and brush both sides of the bread with olive oil. Cook until charred with stripes on both sides. If your figs aren't ripe and juicy, now's the time to chargrill them, too.

To serve, thickly spread the toast with the chilled creamed feta, top with the fig halves and drizzle with honey. Serve immediately.

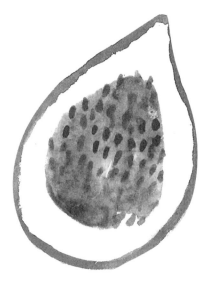

Shop-bought yoghurt and labna (yoghurt cheese) can be wonderful, but making these voluptuous ingredients from scratch is simple and strangely satisfying – strange because there really isn't much to do. I have a batch of DIY yoghurt on the go most of the time because it's delicious, healthy and endlessly useful in Mediterranean cooking. Use full-cream milk for optimum lusciousness.

Greek-style yoghurt and labna

Serves 6–8

2 litres (70 fl oz/8 cups) full-cream (whole) milk
100 g (3½ oz) plain active yoghurt, at room temperature

Pour the milk into a saucepan and slowly heat until almost – but not quite – simmering. Remove from the heat and cool until you can bear dipping your (clean) finger in – this will take about 20 minutes. Scoop a few tablespoons of the milk into the yoghurt and stir, then pour the milky yoghurt back into the saucepan and mix well. Cover and wrap the pan in a tea towel to help the milk stay warm.

Switch on the oven light (not the oven!), place the pan inside, and leave for 4–8 hours or until the mixture has thickened to a yoghurty consistency. Or just leave the pan in a warm place for up to 12 hours.

The yoghurt tastes delicious like this but to make thick and creamy Greek-style yoghurt, line a colander set over a bowl with a piece of muslin (cheesecloth). Tip in the yoghurt, fold the fabric over to cover, and leave to drain for several hours until thick and creamy.

Use the yoghurt as it is or try one of my favourite toppings:

- pomegranate seeds, pomegranate molasses and walnuts
- olive oil, dates, sunflower seeds, orange zest and a pinch of salt.

To turn the yoghurt into labna, gather together the edges of the cloth and tie with a long piece of string. Suspend the bundle over a bowl in the fridge, tied to one of the shelves or, if the bowl is deep enough for the bundle to dangle, attach the bundle to a wooden spoon set over the bowl. Leave for 2–3 days – the whey will drip into the bowl, so the longer you leave it the thicker the labna will be. Unwrap and observe the gorgeous pattern made by the fabric. Serve the labna immediately on bread or:

- roll tablespoonfuls into balls and roll in herbs or spices like chives or za'atar, then store in a jar and submerge in olive oil
- stir in a spoonful of dark brown sugar and serve as an alternative to cream with poached fruit such as quince or rhubarb.

Cherries and basil parked in the same bowl might seem a bit odd, but it's a lovely combination, and a healthy one – a plate that's as beautiful as it is delicious. If you're lucky enough to have very ripe and juicy cherries, you might not need all the honey here. You could make this more substantial by spreading the labna on toast and spooning the cherries on top.

Stewed cherries with basil and labna

Serves 2

500 g (1 lb 2 oz) sweet
    cherries, pitted
3 tablespoons honey, or
    to taste
3 tablespoons lemon juice
8 basil leaves
4 generous spoonfuls of labna
    (page 24)
white or black sesame seeds,
    for sprinkling

Put the cherries, honey and lemon juice in a saucepan and lightly crush the fruit with a potato masher. Bring to a gentle simmer over medium heat, stirring, then reduce the heat to low, cover and cook for 5 minutes. Remove the lid and simmer for 5 minutes or until the juices turn syrupy.

Remove the pan from the heat, tear the basil leaves and stir into the cherry mixture. Spoon into two bowls, top with the labna and sprinkle with sesame seeds.

This barely constitutes a recipe but somehow the result is so much lovelier than just a simple plate of fruit. It's a fresh, delicious and not to mention pretty way to start the day. Make sure you allow a little time for the plates to sit before serving so that the flavours can mingle – it doesn't take long.

Citrus and cinnamon compote

Serves 4

4 pink grapefruit
4 blood oranges
1 teaspoon caster (superfine) sugar, or to taste
½ teaspoon ground cinnamon, or to taste
finely grated zest of 1 lime

Peel the grapefruit and oranges with a sharp knife, making sure you remove all the bitter white pith. Working over a bowl to catch the juices, cut between the membranes of the fruit to remove the segments. Arrange the segments on serving plates as you go – there's one grapefruit and one orange per person.

Give the juices you've captured a little stir, then spoon some over each plate. Sprinkle each serving with a little sugar, cinnamon and lime zest. Set the plates aside and then go about your business for 20 minutes before serving.

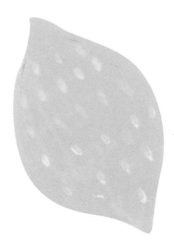

Yoghurt & cheese

A Mediterranean table without dairy is unthinkable. A splodge of Greek yoghurt, its rich sourness tempered with fruit, nuts and a drizzle of honey, is breakfast nirvana for me. Feta crumbled over salad, pasta or grilled meat delivers a salty hit that I often crave, especially when the weather is hot. Ricotta spread thickly on toast, served with a punchy salad, makes a refreshing light meal. Yoghurt and cheese are staples in the Mediterranean – but traditionally served in moderation, adorning other ingredients.

I often substitute yoghurt for mayonnaise, or whisk it with olive oil and lemon juice to make a lovely thick dressing. It makes its way into sauces, too, as a thickener instead of cream – but cooked over moderate heat as it can curdle when approaching boiling point. Yoghurt also adds lightness and tang to baking.

Fresh cheeses such as feta, mozzarella and ricotta are best enjoyed simply, just thrown together with fruit, vegetables, nuts and seeds. For firmer cheeses, such as haloumi and kefalotyri, I like to draw out the flavour with a little heat. I happily nibble on some parmesan or pecorino while I'm cooking – chef's privilege – and these harder cheeses are ideal for grating and adding a umami flavour bomb to other robust ingredients.

As ever, it's best to buy the good stuff if you're not making your own. Look for Greek-style yoghurt that contains gut-friendly live cultures, and buy fresh cheeses that are as fresh as possible – they will turn rancid quickly. When it comes to full fat versus low fat, the choice is yours, but I buy the former. Recent research strongly suggests that full-fat dairy might not be as bad for your waistline or your health as previously thought. Fats in yoghurt and cheese are also believed to aid in the absorption of nutritious lycopene in tomatoes, as well as vitamins A, D, E and K. Full-fat dairy is certainly more satisfying and it keeps you feeling full for longer. It's also more delicious. And that's what counts.

These scrumptious little flat pies are based on the Cretan *mizithropita*, traditionally made with mizithra cheese, sometimes difficult to find outside Greece. Here I've made them with labna but you can use goat's cheese or even ricotta. Whatever you use, make sure you leave time for the cheese balls to firm up in the fridge before you cook the pies.

Crispy cheese pies with honey and za'atar

Makes 6

250 g (9 oz/1⅔ cups) plain
   (all-purpose) flour
a pinch of fine sea salt
¼ teaspoon bicarbonate
   of soda (baking soda)
1 egg, lightly beaten
2 tablespoons olive oil, plus
   extra for oiling
150 g (5½ oz) labna (page 24),
   soft goat's cheese or ricotta
   cheese
honey, for drizzling
za'atar or ground cinnamon,
   for sprinkling

Whisk together the flour, salt and bicarbonate of soda. Make a well in the centre, pour in the egg and olive oil and stir with a wooden spoon. Gradually add about 100 ml (3½ fl oz) water to make a sticky dough. Tip out onto a well-oiled work surface and knead for a couple of minutes until smooth and supple. Don't add flour – the more you knead, the less the dough will stick and it needs to remain a little wet. Lightly oil a mixing bowl, add the dough and turn to coat. Cover the dough with a clean tea towel and set aside for 30 minutes to allow the gluten time to develop.

Meanwhile, divide the cheese into six equal portions and roll each portion into a ball. Chill until needed.

When the dough is ready, divide it into six equal pieces. Using damp hands, roll each piece into a ball, place on an oiled work surface and cover with a clean tea towel. Flatten one of the dough balls into a 10 cm (4 inch) disc. Place a cheese ball in the middle of the dough, gather the edges of the dough together to cover the cheese and then pinch to seal. Place the parcel, seam side down, on the work surface and gently press into a 15 cm (6 inch) circle with your fingers, working out from the centre.

Set a non-stick frying pan over medium–high heat and lightly brush with olive oil. Place one cheese-filled disc in the pan and cook for 2–3 minutes on each side or until slightly puffed and golden. Serve immediately, or wrap in a tea towel to keep warm while you repeat with the rest of the dough. You can assemble the next cheese-filled disc while one is cooking, so you get a little production line going.

Serve the pies warm, drizzled with honey and sprinkled with za'atar or cinnamon.

Tomatoes grown in the Mediterranean are so glorious and abundant, it makes sense that every region has its own way of serving them simply with bread to soak up all the sun-sweetened juices. This is my version, and it's completely delicious. Take it as read that if you aren't in possession of wonderfully ripe tomatoes, you should give this recipe a miss until you are.

Tomato bread with mint, hazelnuts and jamon

Makes 6 slices

3 large ripe tomatoes
1 large handful chopped
  mint leaves, plus extra
  leaves to serve
sea salt flakes
freshly ground black pepper
6 slices Olive oil bread
  (page 19), sourdough or
  country-style bread
olive oil, for brushing
1 garlic clove, cut in half
6 slices jamon
1 handful skinned hazelnuts,
  toasted and roughly chopped
hazelnut oil or olive oil, to serve

Slice the tops off the tomatoes and grate them over a bowl using the largest holes of a box grater. Discard the skins. You'll end up with a nice juicy pulp. Add the mint and generously season with sea salt and black pepper. Stir and set to one side while you get on with the rest of the dish.

Lightly brush the bread with olive oil and cook on a hot chargrill pan or barbecue until striped on both sides. Lightly rub the hot toast with the cut sides of the garlic clove. Go easy – you want just a hint of garlic.

Arrange the toast on a large platter and generously spoon the minty tomato pulp over it. Arrange curls of jamon on top and sprinkle with the hazelnuts and extra mint leaves. Drizzle with hazelnut oil or olive oil and serve immediately.

This is a superb breakfast – the fact that it contains a hefty serve of health-giving greens is just an added bonus. The mix of greens suggested below is simply what I often have to hand, but you can experiment with other variations. This is also a great way to use up bits and bobs in the salad crisper – just make sure you thinly slice the greens and remove any tough stalks. See the section on leafy greens on page 156 for other ideas.

Baked eggs with greens, avocado and yoghurt

Serves 2–4

2 tablespoons olive oil
250 g (9 oz) mixed greens
  such as kale, spring greens,
  wild garlic, savoy cabbage,
  beetroot greens, turnip tops
  and parsley, thinly sliced
sea salt flakes
freshly ground black pepper
2 garlic cloves, finely chopped
60–125 ml (2–4 fl oz/¼–½ cup)
  chicken or vegetable stock
a pinch of Aleppo pepper or
  chilli flakes
4 eggs
1 avocado, sliced
3 tablespoons Greek-style
  yoghurt
smoked paprika, for sprinkling

Preheat the oven to 180°C (350°F).

Warm the olive oil in an ovenproof frying pan over medium–high heat and add the mixed greens, handful by handful, stirring and allowing them to wilt as you go. It might seem like you have too many greens but don't worry, they will cook down. Season with sea salt and black pepper, then stir-fry for a couple of minutes until all the greens have softened slightly. Add the garlic and a splash of the stock, then continue to stir-fry for a couple more minutes until the leaves are tender. Add as much stock as you need to prevent the greens drying out and sticking to the pan, but you don't want any liquid left when the greens are cooked.

Remove the pan from the heat and stir in the Aleppo pepper or chilli flakes. Make four indentations in the greens and crack an egg into each one, then arrange the avocado slices around the eggs. Stir the yoghurt well to loosen it, then spoon it in blobs over the greens and sprinkle with paprika.

Bake for about 10 minutes or until the egg whites are just set and the yolks are still runny. Serve immediately, accompanied by some good bread, if you like.

This is one of those recipes I cook again and again, especially when I have several mouths to feed at breakfast or brunch. The fact that it only requires one pan is good enough reason for me, but it's also hearty, healthy and much more tasty than your standard fry-up. While I'm partial to a baked bean, chickpeas are more delicious when they're spiced and simmered in delicious juices like this. If you want to cook them from scratch, I salute you, but don't feel guilty about using tinned – life's too short. A word of warning: harissa paste can vary in its spiciness, with some brands much hotter than others. If you definitely don't like heat, add the harissa gradually and taste as you go – you can always stir in a little more at the end.

One-pan breakfast with Merguez sausages, eggs and chickpeas

Serves 4 generously

1 tablespoon olive oil
400 g (14 oz) Merguez
   sausages, thickly sliced
480 g (1 lb 1 oz) cooked
   chickpeas or 2 x 400 g
   (14 oz) tins chickpeas,
   rinsed and drained
300 g (10½ oz) cherry
   tomatoes, halved
200 ml (7 fl oz) tomato passata
1–3 teaspoons harissa paste,
   or to taste (see note above)
a squeeze of lime
sea salt flakes
freshly ground black pepper
4–6 eggs
a scattering of oregano leaves,
   to serve
country-style bread, to serve

Warm the oil in a frying pan and add the sliced sausages. Fry over medium–high heat, shaking the pan frequently, for 5 minutes or until brown all over. Add the chickpeas and cook for another minute, shaking the pan to coat in the spicy sausage oil. Add the tomatoes, passata and harissa paste, and mix well. Reduce the heat to low, cover (use a baking tray if your frying pan doesn't have a lid) and cook for 5 minutes or until the tomatoes are just tender but still holding their shape. Add the squeeze of lime and some sea salt and black pepper to taste.

Remove the pan from the heat, make indentations in the mixture and crack an egg into each one. Return the pan to medium heat, cover and cook until the eggs are done to your liking. I like mine with firmish whites and runny yolks, which takes about 6 minutes.

Sprinkle with oregano, then take the pan to the table to serve. Chunks of bread to dunk in the tomatoey juices are mandatory.

Plates to share

These neat little bites might look a bit fussy presentation-wise, but when nature provides her own crockery it makes sense to use it. The key to the success of this dish is to chop everything very finely so the flavours really mingle and you get lots of each ingredient in every bite.

Witlof cups with almond tabouleh

Serves 4–6

45 g (1½ oz) flaked almonds
1 tablespoon sesame seeds
1 generous handful flat-leaf
    parsley leaves, finely chopped
40 g (1½ oz) red onion, finely
    chopped
15 g (½ oz) dried cranberries,
    finely chopped
½ red apple
about 12 witlof (chicory) leaves

For the dressing

3 tablespoons olive oil
30 ml (1 fl oz) red wine vinegar
1 teaspoon honey
1 teaspoon ras el hanout
sea salt
freshly ground black pepper

Briefly toast the almonds and sesame seeds in a dry frying pan, shaking frequently, until they take on a little colour and smell lovely. Watch carefully as they can burn easily. Pull the pan off the heat and put to one side.

Next, make the dressing. Simply put all of the ingredients in a screw-top jar and shake until combined.

Combine the parsley, onion and cranberries in a bowl and toss. Finely chop the cooled nuts and seeds to make a nutty rubble and add to the bowl. Dice the apple very finely, leaving the skin on as it adds lovely colour, and add this too (don't chop it any earlier or it will turn brown).

Add the dressing to the tabouleh a spoonful at a time, tossing well after each addition. Stop adding the dressing when the tabouleh is coated (you might not need it all). Taste and add more salt and pepper if needed.

Scoop a couple of teaspoons of the tabouleh mixture into each witlof leaf and arrange artfully on a platter if you feel inclined. Serve immediately.

This cooling, flavourful pot of pastel loveliness is delicious served as part of a mezze, scooped up in warm pitta bread like the traditional cucumber version. It also makes a terrific sauce to go with roast meats (try it with the Yoghurt-marinated lamb on page 96) and alongside fish. It's important to use strained goat's milk yoghurt, not the thinner unstrained stuff. If you can't find it, just strain normal goat's milk yoghurt through a coffee filter or a strainer lined with muslin (cheesecloth) until thickened. If that's too much faff, use Greek-style yoghurt, but the flavour won't be quite so wonderful.

Chunky fennel and radish tzatziki

Serves 4

120 g (4¼ oz) fennel bulb
   with fronds
160 g (5½ oz) radishes
250 g (9 oz) strained goat's
   milk yoghurt
2 garlic cloves, crushed
2 tablespoons extra virgin
   olive oil
3 tablespoons lemon juice
1 small handful dill, chopped
1 small handful mint leaves,
   chopped
sea salt flakes
freshly ground black pepper
warm pitta bread, to serve

Chop the fennel fronds and set aside. Grate the fennel bulb and radishes on the largest holes of a box grater. Place the grated fennel and radishes in a clean tea towel and squeeze out any excess liquid.

Combine the yoghurt, garlic, olive oil and lemon juice in a bowl and mix well. Add the grated fennel and radishes along with the chopped dill, mint and fennel fronds. Stir to combine, then taste and add sea salt and black pepper if needed. Cover with plastic wrap and chill for a couple of hours for the flavours to develop.

Serve the tzatziki with warm pitta bread for scooping.

As much as I love the traditional chickpea and tahini hummus, I like to shake up the flavours once in a while, and this version is wonderful. The vibrant yellow colour is from the turmeric, which many people think of as an Indian spice for curries, but it is also widely used in the eastern Mediterranean where it's known as 'poor man's saffron'. With its intriguing flavour and health benefits (it's one of the most nutritious foods), turmeric is a bit of a spice star.

Pine nut hummus with figs and walnuts

Serves 2–4

400 g (14 oz) tinned chickpeas
4 tablespoons pine nuts,
  lightly toasted
½ small garlic clove
1 tablespoon olive oil
2 tablespoons lemon juice,
  or to taste
2 tablespoons Greek-style
  yoghurt
½ teaspoon ground cumin
½ teaspoon ground turmeric
sea salt flakes
freshly ground black pepper
2 soft dried figs, finely chopped
1 very small handful walnuts,
  lightly toasted and chopped
walnut oil, for drizzling
warm pitta bread and vegetable
  crudités, to serve

Drain the chickpeas, keeping the liquid from the tin. Weigh the chickpeas – you will need 160 g (5½ oz) – then rinse and drain.

Tip the pine nuts into a food processor and blitz to a paste. Add the chickpeas to the pine nuts along with the garlic, olive oil, lemon juice, yoghurt, cumin, turmeric and sea salt, and blitz until smooth. Add enough of the chickpea liquid to make the mixture voluptuous and creamy, then have a taste and add more salt, lemon juice or some black pepper if you like.

Scrape the hummus into a shallow bowl and top with the figs, walnuts and a drizzle of walnut oil. Serve with warm pitta bread and vegetables for scooping and dipping.

This is like a classic beetroot, goat's cheese and watercress salad but in purée form – each mouthful is deeply flavourful, earthy and a little bit sharp. It's very more-ish. Goat's milk yoghurt isn't hard to find but if you use plain Greek-style yoghurt this will still be delicious.

Beetroot, goat's yoghurt and watercress purée

Serves 4

600 g (1 lb 5 oz) raw beetroot
75 ml (2¼ fl oz) olive oil
1 teaspoon nigella seeds
sea salt flakes
freshly ground black pepper
30 ml (1 fl oz) balsamic vinegar
200 g (7 oz/¾ cup) goat's milk
 yoghurt
60 g (2¼ oz/2 cups) watercress
 leaves, chopped
40 g (1½ oz/⅓ cup) toasted
 walnuts, roughly chopped
lemon juice, to taste
vegetable crudités, toast or
 crackers, to serve

Trim and peel the beetroot, then chop it into 2 cm (¾ inch) cubes (accuracy isn't make-or-break here but the cubes should be roughly the same size).

Heat 2 tablespoons of the olive oil in a saucepan over medium–high heat. Add the beetroot and nigella seeds, and generously season with sea salt and black pepper. Stir to coat the beetroot in the oil for a minute or so. Add the balsamic vinegar and let it bubble up for a moment, then reduce the heat to low, cover and cook until the beetroot is very tender, about 30–40 minutes. Stir and take a peek now and then, adding a splash of water if the beetroot looks like it might stick to the bottom of the pan.

When the beetroot is very tender, set it aside to cool a little, then transfer to a food processor and blitz with the remaining olive oil until the mixture is as smooth as you can get it. Add the yoghurt, watercress, walnuts, a splash of lemon juice and some more salt and pepper. Blitz until the purée is lovely and creamy – this could take quite a few minutes depending on the power of your food processor, so stick with it. Taste and add some more salt, pepper or lemon juice if needed.

Serve the purée with vegetables for dipping, or spread it thickly on toast or crackers.

I try to love traditional tapenade – the punchy version from the south of France – but secretly I've always found it a little harsh and bitter. This version is much more addictive. The figs take the edge off the pungency of the olives and capers, without making the final result overly sweet. Play around with the proportions, if you like, adding more capers or olives to get the balance of flavour just the way you like it.

Fig, almond and olive tapenade

Makes 1 small pot

40 g (1½ oz/¼ cup) blanched
   almonds
1 teaspoon fennel seeds
200 g (7 oz) soft dried figs
160 g (5½ oz) pitted kalamata
   olives, or to taste
1 tablespoon capers, or to
   taste, rinsed
35 ml (1 fl oz) balsamic vinegar
2 tablespoons olive oil
¼ teaspoon dried oregano
crackers or cheese, to serve

Put the almonds and fennel seeds in a dry frying pan and toast for a few minutes until fragrant and the nuts start to take on a little colour. Transfer to a bowl to cool.

Meanwhile, blitz the figs to a rough paste in a food processor, then add the remaining ingredients along with the cooled almonds and fennel seeds. Blitz to form a rough, well-combined paste. Have a taste and add more capers or olives if you like.

Serve the tapenade with crackers or cheese.

Olive oil

Olive oil is the cornerstone of Mediterranean cooking. From the herby, earthy varieties produced in Greece to the bright-green grassy elixirs of Tuscany, olive oil is a delicious and health-giving staple that I couldn't live without in my kitchen.

Made from nothing more than the pressed juice of olives, the flavour and colour of olive oil varies from region to region, sometimes from hillside to hillside, according to the olive variety, the terroir and the producer. And with this variety comes versatility. I pour olive oil into everything from dressings and sauces to cake batters and bread doughs, and also use it for drizzling, dipping and frying. It lubricates, seasons and delivers crispness – it's amazing stuff.

Extra virgin olive oil, the best quality, is made from the first cold pressings of the finest olives, and therefore has the lowest acidity and fullest flavour. Some people think cooking with extra virgin olive oil is wasteful because some of the flavour is lost in the heat. But it's worth considering how poorer quality oils are made.

Simple olive oils and lower-grade virgin olive oils are sometimes extracted using solvents, treated with heat or diluted with cheaper oils. That's why I tend to use extra virgin for everything, but keep different kinds to hand for different uses.

The finest (and often priciest) extra virgin oils are best reserved for drizzling over vegetables and soup, or dunking bread into, so that you can fully savour the flavour you're paying for. Lesser quality extra virgin oils, often golden and mildly flavoured, are best for cooking and using in delicate sauces or wherever you don't want their flavour to overshadow other ingredients. Often the choice is yours – I love a bold olive oil flavour in cakes, but you might prefer it milder.

The issue of dietary fat has been debated for decades and remains controversial. But when it comes to olive oil, most experts agree that it's one of the healthiest. Not only does it contain modest levels of vitamins E and K, but it is also loaded with antioxidants, some of which have powerful health benefits. I know one prominent cardiologist in the UK who describes extra virgin olive oil as a 'medicine' and recommends consuming at least 3 tablespoons each day.

Place a bowl of this in front of me with a pile of crackers or bread and I'm gone – I'll just scoff the lot. I love the mash-up of sweet, sour and lemony flavours against the rich tomato sauce. This makes a delicious and easy starter for a crowd: make a batch in advance and chargrill some good bread, brushed with olive oil, to make bruschetta. It's also lovely with the Semolina and olive oil crackers from page 53.

Lemon thyme and tomato jam

Makes about 300 g (10½ oz)

8 ripe tomatoes, about 800 g
    (1 lb 12 oz), halved
2 tablespoons olive oil, plus
    extra for oiling
1 red onion, halved and thinly
    sliced
1 garlic clove, crushed
2 tablespoons honey
3 tablespoons sherry vinegar
sea salt flakes
freshly ground black pepper
2 tablespoons lemon thyme
    leaves

Preheat the grill (broiler) to high. Put the tomatoes, cut side down, on an oiled baking tray with a rim. Cook until the skins start to blister and blacken, about 10 minutes. When the tomatoes are cool enough to handle, slip off the skins – they have probably started to slide off anyway – and roughly chop the flesh and the charred skins, making sure you catch all the juices. Set aside.

Heat the olive oil in a saucepan and gently fry the red onion until softened, about 8 minutes. Add the crushed garlic and the chopped tomatoes, and cook for 5 minutes more. Stir in the honey and sherry vinegar, and season with sea salt and black pepper. Cook for another 5 minutes, then remove from the heat and stir in the lemon thyme. Have a taste and add a little more salt or pepper if you like.

If you see zucchini blossoms at the greengrocer's, grab them (or better still, pick some if you grow zucchini). I love their fresh and delicate flavour. There are two types of flower: the one with the cute immature vegetable attached is the female, while the one with the long thin stalk is the male that is more commonly used in cooking. I've used the female but if you only have male flowers, never fear – just find yourself a zucchini as well. Start by making a batch of the pitta bread dough from page 20. You can begin making the sauce once you have set the balls aside to rise for 30 minutes.

Flatbreads with zucchini blossoms and ricotta

Makes 8

1 quantity Pillowy pitta bread
  dough (page 20)
16 female zucchini (courgette)
  flowers or 16 male flowers
  plus 1 large zucchini
250 g (9 oz) ricotta cheese
olive oil, for drizzling
1 handful basil leaves
1 handful mint leaves

For the tomato sauce

400 ml (14 fl oz) tomato
  passata
2 garlic cloves, crushed
1 tablespoon olive oil
sea salt flakes
freshly ground black pepper

Roll the pitta bread dough into eight balls and set aside to prove for 30 minutes as instructed in the recipe.

While this is happening, preheat the oven to 220°C (425°F) and line a large baking tray with baking paper.

Make the tomato sauce by stirring together the passata, garlic, olive oil and lots of sea salt and black pepper in a bowl. Set to one side.

If you are using female zucchini flowers, cut off the baby vegetables 1 cm (½ inch) or so below the flower and trim the base. Gently open out the flower trumpets and pinch out the stamens. Slice the baby zucchini into ribbons with a vegetable peeler. If using male flowers, slice the whole zucchini into ribbons.

Using a lightly floured work surface, roll each dough ball into a thick disc about 25 cm (10 inches) in diameter and put on the baking tray (you will need to roll and cook these in batches). Prick the dough with a fork and spread the tomato sauce over the top, leaving a 2 cm (¾ inch) border. Scatter with some of the zucchini ribbons. Place two zucchini flowers in the middle, spoon the ricotta over the zucchini ribbons and drizzle with a little olive oil. Bake for 12–14 minutes or until the crust is golden.

Serve the flatbreads immediately, sprinkled with the herbs.

I can hear you asking, 'Why would I want to make my own crackers?' All I can say is they're easy and delicious, and can be whipped up when the cupboard is virtually bare. I've suggested goat's cheese to adorn them, but obviously you can use whatever you have. They're also nice crumbled into hot soup or even eaten on their own: the semolina gives them a crumbly crunch.

Semolina and olive oil crackers with whipped goat's cheese

Makes about 20

130 g (4½ oz/⅔ cup) fine semolina
90 g (3¼ oz) plain (all-purpose) flour, plus extra for rolling
½ teaspoon fine sea salt
2 tablespoons olive oil, plus extra for brushing
90 ml (3 fl oz) warm water
dried herbs or salt for sprinkling, such as sea salt flakes, za'atar, dried oregano or truffle salt

For the whipped goat's cheese

200 g (7 oz) soft fresh goat's cheese
3 tablespoons Greek-style yoghurt
finely grated zest of ½ lemon

Preheat the oven to 180°C (350°F) and line a large baking tray with baking paper.

Whisk together the semolina, flour and fine sea salt in a bowl. Stir in the olive oil and then add enough of the warm water to form a not-too-sticky dough. Bring the mixture together with your hands, turn out onto a lightly floured work surface and briefly knead until the dough can be rolled out without crumbling.

Roll the dough out to a thickness of about 3 mm (⅛ inch). I find the easiest way to do this is to place the dough between two pieces of baking paper. Use a cookie cutter or small glass dipped in flour to stamp out discs of dough – I use a 6 cm (2½ inch) cutter to make about 20 crackers. Transfer to the baking tray.

Brush the discs with olive oil and sprinkle with whatever herbs or salt you fancy. Bake for about 8 minutes or until the crackers are pale gold, rotating the tray halfway through cooking. Slide onto a wire rack to cool.

While the crackers are cooling, make the whipped goat's cheese. Beat together the goat's cheese, yoghurt and lemon zest.

Pop spoonfuls of the whipped goat's cheese on top of the cooled crackers to serve.

Potato is generally the foundation of a frittata but chewy and nutty barley is a lovely and healthy alternative. You could use any whole grain you like here – wheat grain and farro are other Mediterranean staples that work well. The grains really absorb the flavour of the melted haloumi, a salty sheep and goat's milk cheese that I can't seem to get enough of. If you can't find sorrel, replace it with the same quantity of baby English spinach or rocket (arugula), tossed with a squeeze of lemon.

Barley, haloumi and sorrel frittata

Serves 4–6

70 g (2½ oz/⅓ cup) pearl barley
75 ml (2¼ fl oz) olive oil
1 red onion, chopped
sea salt flakes
3 garlic cloves
4 eggs, lightly beaten
25 g (1 oz/1 bunch) sorrel, thinly sliced
1 large handful oregano leaves, chopped
1 large handful mint leaves, chopped
grated zest of ½ lemon
250 g (9 oz) haloumi cheese, grated
freshly ground black pepper
180 g (6 oz) Greek-style yoghurt

Cook the barley until tender, according to the packet instructions, then drain well and fluff with a fork. Set aside.

Meanwhile, heat 30 ml (1 fl oz) of the olive oil in a frying pan and fry the onion with a pinch of sea salt until soft and golden, about 8 minutes. Thinly slice two of the garlic cloves, add to the onion and cook for a few minutes more. Pull the pan off the heat.

In a large mixing bowl, combine the eggs with most of the sorrel, the herbs, lemon zest, cooked barley, cooked onion and haloumi. Generously season with sea salt and black pepper.

Preheat the grill (broiler) to high.

Heat 30 ml (1 fl oz) of the remaining oil in a 20 cm (8 inch) ovenproof frying pan and pour in the frittata mixture. Cook over medium–high heat until set at the edges and starting to firm in the centre. Take a peek underneath to check that the bottom is golden – if not, cook a little more.

Place the pan under the grill and cook until the centre of the frittata is just set. Run your knife around the edge of the pan, then carefully invert onto a plate.

Grate the remaining garlic clove into the yoghurt and stir. Add the remaining 3 teaspoons oil and the remaining sorrel, and season with sea salt and black pepper.

Serve the frittata warm or at room temperature with a spoonful of the garlic yoghurt.

We cook these fragrant lamb bites on the barbecue when the weather obliges, which makes this a super-easy dish, as you don't even need to use a pan. I find the trick is to not turn the koftas until they've started to caramelise underneath, or they will stick. It's also wise to buy lamb that has quite a bit of fat in it – or get the butcher to mince up some fatty lamb shoulder for you – so that the koftas are lovely and juicy.

Koftas with sour cherries and tahini dressing

Serves 4

500 g (1 lb 2 oz) minced (ground) lamb
1 onion, chopped
1 small handful mint leaves (about 15 leaves)
2 marjoram sprigs
1 teaspoon ground cumin
1 teaspoon ras el hanout
½ teaspoon ground allspice
½ teaspoon chilli flakes
2 garlic cloves
sea salt flakes
freshly ground black pepper
30 g (1 oz) pine nuts, lightly toasted
25 g (1 oz) dried sour cherries, roughly chopped

For the tahini dressing

2 tablespoons tahini
2 tablespoons lemon juice, or to taste
½ garlic clove, crushed
1 tablespoon Greek-style yoghurt
sea salt flakes
freshly ground black pepper

Put the lamb, onion, herbs, spices and garlic in a food processor and generously season with sea salt and black pepper. Blitz until the mixture is almost a paste, then transfer to a mixing bowl. Toss in the pine nuts and cherries, and mix with your hands until well incorporated. Cover with plastic wrap and refrigerate until you are ready to cook the koftas – ideally at least an hour, to give the flavours time to mingle.

Meanwhile, put the dressing ingredients in a screw-top jar, add 2 tablespoons cold water and shake until combined and creamy. Have a taste and add more lemon juice or salt and pepper, or a bit more water to get it to the right consistency. Set to one side.

Divide the kofta mixture into eight equal portions and roll each one into an oval. Thread onto metal skewers – you should be able to fit two koftas on each. Cook on a hot chargrill pan or barbecue for 3–4 minutes, then turn and cook the other side for a similar time. Don't be tempted to turn the koftas before they have caramelised underneath or they will stick.

Serve the koftas immediately, with the tahini dressing alongside, stuffed into flatbreads with salad, if you fancy.

Spaniards and Italians have been producing salt-cured tuna for centuries (the fish is known as *mojama* in Spain and *mosciame* in Italy). They cure loins of tuna in salt for a few days, then rinse the fish and dry them in the Mediterranean sun and breeze for two to three weeks. The result packs a superb umami punch.

Cured tuna with almonds and cucumber salsa

Serves 4

125 g (4½ oz) salt-cured tuna,
  thinly sliced
1 spring onion (scallion),
  thinly sliced
40 g (1½ oz/¼ cup) blanched
  almonds (ideally Marcona
  almonds)

For the dressing

3 tablespoons extra virgin
  olive oil
1 tablespoon sherry vinegar
sea salt
freshly ground black pepper

For the salsa

½ cucumber, peeled, seeded
  and finely chopped
1 red capsicum (pepper),
  finely chopped
2 ripe but firm tomatoes,
  seeded and finely chopped
2 chervil sprigs, chopped

Start by making the dressing. In a small bowl, whisk together the olive oil and sherry vinegar with a little sea salt and black pepper and set to one side.

For the salsa, combine the cucumber, capsicum, tomatoes and chervil in a salad bowl and toss with 2 tablespoons of the dressing.

Divide the salsa among four serving plates and top with the tuna, spring onion and almonds. Drizzle with a little more of the dressing and serve immediately.

There are quite a few options when it comes to serving these lovely bites, which is why I cook them so often. They make fantastic canapés, spiked with toothpicks and drizzled with some of the sauce, or I sometimes do them as a help-yourself dish for a tapas-style spread. If I've been domestic goddessy and stashed some in the freezer (cooked and ready to be reheated on a tray under some foil in the oven), I serve them as a main with pasta or grains – rice, spelt and barley are delicious – and some greens.

Eggplant and pistachio bites with spicy tomato sauce

Makes 24

1 large eggplant (aubergine), about 450 g (1 lb)
70 ml (2¼ fl oz) olive oil, plus extra for brushing
sea salt flakes
freshly ground black pepper
2 garlic cloves
60 g (2¼ oz) bread, blitzed into soft crumbs in a food processor, plus extra if needed
2 tablespoons chopped mint leaves
2 tablespoons chopped oregano leaves
30 g (1 oz) parmesan cheese, grated
1 egg yolk
finely grated zest of ½ lemon
3 tablespoons pistachio nuts, toasted and chopped reasonably fine
500 ml (17 fl oz/2 cups) tomato passata
1 tablespoon balsamic vinegar
½ teaspoon smoked paprika

Preheat the oven to 200°C (400°F). Cut the eggplant lengthways into quarters and place in a roasting tin. Toss with 2 tablespoons of the olive oil and generously season with sea salt and black pepper. Bake for 30 minutes or until the eggplant is charred on top and very soft. Set aside until cool enough to handle, then finely chop – include the skins, which should be tender. Transfer to a strainer set over a bowl and gently press with the back of a spoon to release all the excess liquid. This step is really important, or the bites won't hold together. Leave the oven on, as you will use it again to cook the bites.

Tip the eggplant into a mixing bowl. Crush one of the garlic cloves and add it to the bowl, along with the breadcrumbs, herbs, parmesan, egg yolk, lemon zest and pistachios. Season with salt and pepper, and mix well. The mixture should be firm enough to roll into balls that keep their shape, so add more breadcrumbs if needed. Roll level tablespoons of the mixture into balls with damp hands, and set on an oiled baking tray. Brush the bites with olive oil and bake for 25 minutes or until golden and cooked through.

Meanwhile, warm the remaining olive oil in a saucepan over low heat. Bruise the remaining garlic clove by squashing it with the side of a knife, add it to the pan and fry until slightly coloured, then remove with a slotted spoon. Add the passata, balsamic vinegar and paprika, and season with salt and pepper. Bring to the boil, then reduce the heat and simmer until the sauce is thickened. Have a taste and add some more salt and pepper if you think it needs it.

When cooked, transfer the bites to a shallow serving bowl and pour enough sauce over the top to cover them. Serve the remaining sauce on the side, with grains, pasta or salad.

These delicious little bites, a speciality of Sicily, are traditionally made with risotto rice but I love the nutty flavour and firmer texture of spelt. Here I've filled them with melting mozzarella and they go down a treat served as finger food with drinks, or as a main course with a big bowl of salad alongside. It's no big deal to roll and fry these – assemble them ahead, pop them in the fridge and cook them a few minutes before you're going to eat.

Spelt arancini with mozzarella, porcini and thyme

Makes about 24

50 g (1¾ oz) dried porcini mushrooms
200 ml (7 fl oz) boiling water
700 ml (24 fl oz) chicken or vegetable stock
250 g (9 oz) pearled spelt
50 g (1¾ oz/½ cup) grated parmesan cheese
sea salt flakes
freshly ground black pepper
3 large eggs
2 tablespoons olive oil
1 tablespoon chopped thyme leaves
a pinch of chilli flakes
finely grated zest of ½ lemon, plus a squeeze of lemon juice
1 small garlic clove, finely chopped
100 g (3½ oz/⅔ cup) plain (all-purpose) flour
140 g (5 oz/1¼ cups) dry breadcrumbs
125 g (4½ oz) mozzarella ball, diced
vegetable oil, for deep-frying
lemon wedges, to serve

Soak the porcini in the boiling water for 15 minutes, then drain, keeping the soaking liquid. Squeeze the excess liquid from the porcini, then finely chop and set aside.

Pour the porcini soaking liquid and stock into a saucepan and bring to the boil. Add the spelt, reduce the heat and simmer, stirring now and then, until the stock is completely absorbed and the grains are tender – this should take around 15–20 minutes. Add a splash of water or stock if the liquid is absorbed before the spelt is cooked. When the grains are tender, remove the pan from the heat and stir in the parmesan. Taste for seasoning, adding some sea salt and black pepper if needed, then stir in one of the eggs. Transfer to a shallow bowl and chill for an hour or so to firm up.

Meanwhile, heat the olive oil in a small frying pan, add the porcini, thyme, chilli and lemon zest, and season with salt and pepper. Fry for a few minutes until aromatic. Add the garlic and lemon juice. Cook, stirring, for a few minutes until cooked through. Set aside.

Crack the remaining eggs into a shallow bowl and lightly beat. Spread out the flour and breadcrumbs on separate plates. Season the flour with salt and pepper.

Stir the porcini mixture and mozzarella into the chilled spelt mixture until evenly mixed. Using damp hands, roll a heaped tablespoon of the mixture into a 4.5 cm (1¾ inch) ball, squeezing gently so it keeps its shape. Repeat with the rest of the mixture. Dredge each ball in the flour, dunk in the egg and roll in the breadcrumbs.

Heat the vegetable oil to 170–180°C (325–350°F) or until a small piece of bread tossed into the oil sizzles and turns golden in 30 seconds. Gently lower the spelt balls into the oil and fry in batches until deep golden brown. Remove with a slotted spoon and drain on paper towel. Sprinkle with salt and serve immediately, with lemon wedges.

The fact that these more-ish discs are full of goodness goes over the heads of my children, who love them simply because they taste good. They disappear as quickly as I cook them, clutched in paper towel and gobbled up with a sprinkling of salt and a squeeze of lemon. Enjoy them as finger food or stuff them into pitta bread with some salad for a proper light meal. You can make them ahead and keep them in the fridge until you're ready to cook, which is always a bonus.

Tomato, feta and pistachio fritters

Makes 10

60 g (2¼ oz/⅓ cup) burghul (bulgur)

400 g (14 oz) tomatoes, peeled, seeded and finely chopped

6 sun-dried tomatoes, finely chopped

100 g (3½ oz) feta cheese, crumbled

1 small handful basil leaves, torn

1 small handful mint leaves, chopped

1 teaspoon oregano leaves, chopped

finely grated zest of ½ lemon, plus a squeeze of lemon to serve

2 tablespoons chopped pistachio nuts

40 g (1½ oz/⅔ cup) fresh breadcrumbs

about 75 g (2½ oz/½ cup) plain (all-purpose) flour

1 egg yolk

freshly ground black pepper

olive oil, for frying

sea salt flakes

Put the burghul in a heatproof bowl with just enough boiling water to cover. Cover with plastic wrap and set aside for 20 minutes or until tender and the water has been absorbed. Drain away any remaining liquid and pat dry with paper towel.

In a mixing bowl, combine the burghul, tomatoes, sun-dried tomatoes, feta, herbs, lemon zest, pistachios, breadcrumbs, half the flour, egg yolk and black pepper. Gently mix together until combined – clean hands work well. Now, add enough of the remaining flour to form a mixture that is still quite wet but will hold together as patties. Form the mixture into 10 patties about 8 cm (3¼ inches) wide, transfer to a plate and chill for at least 30 minutes to firm up a little.

Heat a couple of generous splashes of olive oil in a frying pan and cook the fritters in batches for about 4 minutes on each side or until they are golden.

Drain the fritters on paper towel and serve sprinkled with sea salt and a squeeze of lemon. They are also delicious with the Chunky fennel and radish tzatziki (page 42) or Tahini dressing (page 56).

These are delicious parcels and not really any trouble to make – just a little brushing of filo with butter, which I find quite a pleasure. Kefalotyri cheese is fairly easy to find these days: it's a hard, salty sheep's milk cheese from Greece that's rather bland eaten raw but comes into its own when melted to gooey deliciousness, as it is in this recipe. My top tip is not to stint on the mint: it mellows out during cooking and won't taste too strong, I promise.

Cheese, pea and spearmint rolls

Makes 16

400 g (14 oz) kefalotyri cheese (or haloumi will be fine)

2 large handfuls spearmint leaves (garden mint is fine), chopped

½ teaspoon freshly grated nutmeg

finely grated zest of 1 lemon

freshly ground black pepper

sea salt flakes

2 eggs, lightly beaten

80 g (2¾ oz/½ cup) fresh or frozen peas

8 sheets filo pastry (kept in the packet in the fridge until needed)

100 g (3½ oz) butter, melted

2 tablespoons sesame seeds

Preheat the oven to 180°C (350°F) and line a large baking tray with baking paper.

Grate the cheese on the largest holes of a box grater and place in a mixing bowl. Add the mint, nutmeg, lemon zest and pepper and stir together. Taste and add a little salt if necessary – the saltiness of kefalotyri cheese varies widely. Add the eggs and peas, and stir it all together.

Remove the filo from the fridge and cut the sheets in half crossways to make 16 rectangles. Keep the filo between two damp tea towels on your work surface while you work with one piece at a time. Brush the top half of a filo sheet with melted butter. Fold the sheet in half and then brush with more butter. Place 2 heaped tablespoons of the cheese mixture along the bottom edge of the filo, leaving a margin of 2 cm (¾ inch) on each side. Fold in the sides of the filo so they cover the ends of the filling, roll up the parcel and brush the end of the filo with butter to seal the edges. It's important to seal the rolls properly to prevent the cheese leaking. Transfer to the baking tray and repeat with the rest of the filo sheets and cheese mixture.

Brush the rolls with more butter and sprinkle with the sesame seeds. Bake for 25–30 minutes or until the rolls have turned deep gold. Serve hot.

Salads & soups

We almost overdose on *horiatiki* (Greek salad) when we're on holiday in Greece. The combination of salty feta, cooling vegetables and oregano-infused olive oil is perfect to pick at in the heat, but somehow it never quite tastes the same when I try to replicate it at home. Here, I haven't even tried. The classic inspires this version but I've injected some different flavours and herbs. My husband and I disagree on whether feta or ricotta salata is better in this – I prefer the latter for its sharp saltiness but he likes the former for its creaminess. The choice is yours.

Not-so-classic Greek salad

Serves 4 as a side or 2 as a light meal

1 cucumber, about 150 g (5½ oz)
1 red onion, halved
60 g (2¼ oz) mixed radishes
1 large handful mixed cherry tomatoes, halved
40 g (1½ oz/¼ cup) pitted kalamata olives
1 small handful mint leaves, chopped
1 small handful parsley leaves, chopped
1 small handful dill, chopped
200 g (7 oz) feta cheese or ricotta salata

For the dressing

90 ml (3 fl oz) extra virgin olive oil
30 ml (1 fl oz) sherry vinegar
2 teaspoons dried oregano

First, make the dressing. Put the olive oil, vinegar and oregano in a screw-top jar and shake until everything is well combined. Set aside.

Using a vegetable peeler, peel alternate strips off the cucumber skin to create a striped effect. Cut the cucumber in half lengthways, slice into half moons, then place in a large salad bowl. Thinly slice the onion and very thinly slice the radishes (use a mandolin if you have one). Add to the salad bowl along with the tomatoes, olives and herbs, and toss until well combined. Gradually add the dressing, tossing after each addition, until everything is well coated (you might not need it all).

Crumble the feta or ricotta salata over the top and gently fold into the salad, adding more dressing if needed. Serve immediately.

This beautiful salad is similar to coleslaw but the dressing is much lighter and fresher than traditional mayonnaise, which I find a bit too rich and gloopy here. Don't be tempted to grate the vegetables, or the salad will turn mushy – I use a mandolin to thinly slice them, then I cut the slices into matchsticks. Season this salad well – it can take a fair bit of salt.

Matchstick salad with nigella seeds

Serves 4 as a generous side

2 carrots, about 60 g (2¼ oz)
   each, cut into fine matchsticks
160 g (5½ oz) raw beetroot,
   cut into fine matchsticks
2 spring onions (scallions),
   thinly sliced
150 g (5½ oz) celeriac
1 red apple
2 teaspoons nigella seeds

For the dressing

100 g (3½ oz) Greek-style
   yoghurt
finely grated zest and juice
   of ½ lemon, or to taste
1 tablespoon extra virgin
   olive oil
1 garlic clove, crushed
sea salt flakes
freshly ground black pepper

First, make the dressing by whisking together all the ingredients in a small bowl. Have a taste and adjust the seasoning by adding more salt, pepper or lemon juice if needed. Set to one side.

Now, assemble the salad. Pop the carrots, beetroot and spring onions into a salad bowl. Cut the celeriac and apple into fine matchsticks and add these to the bowl too – don't do this earlier or they will turn brown.

Toss enough of the dressing through the salad to coat the vegetables, then fold in the nigella seeds. Have a taste and add more salt, pepper or lemon juice if you like. Set aside for a short time for the flavours to mingle, but no more than 20 minutes or it all goes a bit wet.

It's probably a travesty to say this in a book of Mediterranean recipes, but I'm a bit 'meh' about tabouleh, the traditional herb salad flecked with a teensy bit of burghul (bulgur). I much prefer this version, with pleasingly chewy wheat grain (sometimes known as wheat berries) instead of burghul. Acclaimed chef and Middle Eastern cookery writer Anissa Helou says that when making tabouleh it's important to thinly slice the herbs with a sharp knife and a light hand so as not to turn them to mush. It really does make all the difference.

Wheat grain tabouleh with chervil and mint

Serves 2–4 as a side

70 g (2½ oz) wheat grain
200 g (7 oz) ripe but firm tomatoes (Marmonde are wonderful)
100 g (3½ oz) cucumber, seeds removed, finely diced
2 spring onions (scallions), thinly sliced
2 tablespoons lemon juice, or to taste
2 teaspoons ras el hanout, or to taste
50 g (1¾ oz) very fresh and tender chervil leaves, thinly sliced (parsley is also fine)
15 g (½ oz/¾ cup) mint leaves, thinly sliced
3 tablespoons olive oil
sea salt flakes
freshly ground black pepper

Tip the wheat grain into a saucepan and stir over medium–high heat for a few minutes until you can smell it toasting. Cover with 300 ml (10½ fl oz) water, bring to the boil, then reduce the heat and cover. Cook until the wheat grain is tender – this will depend on the grains, but it might take 30–50 minutes. Rinse in cold running water, spread out on a large plate and pat dry with paper towel. Set aside to cool.

Meanwhile, finely chop the tomatoes and add them to a large bowl, making sure you add all the juices. Add the cucumber, spring onions and the cooled wheat grain. Mix well, then stir in the lemon juice and the ras el hanout.

Fold in the chervil and mint, then the olive oil. Season well with sea salt and black pepper, and add more lemon juice or ras el hanout to taste. The tabouleh can sit for 20 minutes or so to allow the flavours to mingle, but not much longer or the salad will turn soggy.

Oven-dried barley crispbreads called *dakos* or *paximadia* in Greece are traditionally used in this flavourful salad. They are quite hard to find (although you can order them online), so I generally improvise with whatever savoury rusk I can lay my hands on at the supermarket, or I dry out 1 cm (½ inch) thick slices of good-quality bread in a 50°C (120°F) oven for a few hours until hard. The aim is for the hard bread or rusks to soak up all the wonderful tomatoey juices and soften. Needless to say, don't bother with this one unless you have gloriously ripe tomatoes.

Mixed tomato and barley rusk salad with feta and caperberries

Serves 4

4 large ripe tomatoes
24 mixed cherry tomatoes (yellow adds lovely colour), halved
2 tablespoons extra virgin olive oil, plus extra for drizzling
2 tablespoons red wine vinegar
2 tablespoons finely chopped marjoram leaves
finely grated zest of ¼ lemon
¼ teaspoon ground cinnamon
sea salt flakes
freshly ground black pepper
4 Greek barley rusks or dried bread (see note above)
120 g (4¼ oz) feta cheese
40 g (1½ oz/¼ cup) pitted kalamata olives, halved
8 caperberries, sliced

First, get your tomatoes sorted. Slice the tops off the large tomatoes and grate them into a bowl using the largest holes of a box grater. Start with the cut side of the tomatoes against the grater – you will end up with gorgeous scarlet pulp and empty tomato skins, which you discard. Add the cherry tomatoes to the bowl, as well as the oil, red wine vinegar, marjoram, lemon zest and cinnamon. Generously season with sea salt and black pepper, gently toss, then set aside for 10 minutes – ideally in the sunshine – for the flavours to mingle.

Place the rusks or bread on four plates or a large platter and spoon the tomato juices from the bottom of the bowl over them, followed by the tomatoes. Set aside for a further 5 minutes while the bread absorbs the juices.

To serve, crumble the feta over the salad, then scatter the olives and caperberries over the top and drizzle with extra virgin olive oil. Serve immediately.

I know the title of this recipe is a little ... worthy, but in my mind this is temple food of the highest order. The chickpeas and avocado add nutritious substance to otherwise light salad vegetables – I especially love the fresh pop of the peas. As ever, tender fresh peas are best here: it's really not a big deal to pod a few. If you only have frozen peas, that's fine, just tip them into a strainer and pour boiling water over the top – they won't need any more cooking. I sometimes sprinkle garlicky crumbs on top instead of the sesame seeds: just flash-fry some breadcrumbs in olive oil until they turn golden, adding a little crushed garlic and some sea salt flakes towards the end.

Goodness bowl with mint vinaigrette

Serves 4 as a side

40 g (1½ oz) radishes, thinly
    sliced, ideally on a mandolin
2 handfuls baby English spinach
    leaves
50 g (1¾ oz/⅓ cup) freshly
    podded peas (or frozen peas,
    see note above)
2 handfuls pea shoots
1 handful flat-leaf parsley
    leaves
100 g (3½ oz) cooked or tinned
    chickpeas, rinsed and drained
2 avocados
sesame seeds, lightly toasted,
    for sprinkling
nasturtium leaves, to serve
    (optional)

For the dressing

30 ml (1 fl oz) lemon juice,
    or to taste
½ teaspoon dijon mustard
½ garlic clove, crushed
3 tablespoons mild olive oil
12 mint leaves, finely chopped
sea salt flakes
freshly ground black pepper

First, make the dressing. Pop all the ingredients into a screw-top jar and shake until well combined and creamy. Set aside for the flavours to mingle and mellow.

For the salad, combine the radishes, spinach, peas, pea shoots, parsley and chickpeas in a large shallow bowl. Have a taste of the dressing and add more salt, pepper or lemon juice if necessary – it needs to be seasoned well. Gently toss the salad with enough of the dressing to generously coat the vegetables. Halve, stone and slice the avocados. Fold almost all the avocado into the salad.

Scatter the remaining avocado slices over the top of the salad. Drizzle with more dressing, sprinkle with sesame seeds and dot with nasturtium leaves (if using). Serve immediately.

Salty, sweet, tangy and crunchy, this sprightly salad is perfect in the summer when herbs are lush and tender. Use an excellent Italian ricotta if you can – the best ones taste like a creamy cloud, both delicate and rich at the same time. This makes a sublime starter or light lunch on a hot day and is brimming with goodness.

Olive, herb and citrus salad with ricotta toasts

Serves 4

200 g (7 oz) green and black pitted olives, halved if large
1 large handful flat-leaf parsley leaves, about 15 g (½ oz)
1 large handful mint leaves, about 15 g (½ oz), roughly chopped
1 handful tarragon leaves, about 10 g (¼ oz), roughly chopped
3 tablespoons sunflower seeds
1 large lemon
1 large orange
4 large or 8 small slices good-quality country-style bread or Olive oil bread (page 19)
2 tablespoons extra virgin olive oil, plus extra for brushing and drizzling
250 g (9 oz) ricotta cheese
sea salt flakes
freshly ground black pepper

Put the olives, herbs and sunflower seeds in a salad bowl and gently toss to combine.

Peel the lemon and orange with a sharp knife, making sure you remove all of the bitter white pith. Working over a bowl to catch the juices, cut between the membranes of the lemon and orange to remove the segments and add them to the olives and herbs as you go. The segments should be small, so cut any large ones in half lengthways. Gently toss the salad and set aside. Reserve the citrus juices.

Set a chargrill pan over high heat – or ready the barbecue if that's easier – and brush the bread on both sides with olive oil. Cook the bread until charred stripes form on both sides and then thickly spread the toasts with the ricotta.

Add 2 tablespoons of the reserved citrus juices and the 2 tablespoons extra virgin olive oil to the salad bowl and gently toss. Have a taste and add sea salt and black pepper, or more citrus juice or olive oil to taste. Serve immediately, with the ricotta toasts alongside – drizzled with a little extra virgin olive oil if you like.

Milky white lardo – cured pork back fat imbued with herbs and spices – is one of my special treats. It doesn't taste like fat at all, just a melting mouthful that adds a decadent porkiness to all sorts of dishes. I enjoy wafer-thin wisps draped over seafood, bruschetta, pizza, pasta and even warm vegetables. It also works brilliantly as a rich and salty counterpoint to fresh fruit, as here. Just a note: lardo can be quite salty, so watch how much seasoning you add to the dish.

Peach, shaved asparagus and lardo salad

Serves 4

12 asparagus spears
80 g (2¾ oz) rocket (arugula)
    leaves
4 ripe peaches
extra virgin olive oil, for
    brushing
6–8 lardo rashers

For the dressing

90 ml (3 fl oz) fruity extra
    virgin olive oil
30 ml (1 fl oz) lemon juice
sea salt flakes
freshly ground black pepper

Make your dressing first: put the olive oil, lemon juice and a little sea salt and black pepper in a screw-top jar and shake well.

Shave the asparagus into strips with a vegetable peeler. Combine the asparagus and rocket on a serving platter – or individual plates if you like – so they're ready to receive the rest of the ingredients.

Set a large chargrill pan over high heat. While it's heating, halve and stone the peaches, then cut each half into wedges. Lightly brush the cut sides of the peaches with olive oil. Cook the peaches until marked with charred stripes on the cut sides – the flesh should be tender but not soft and falling apart. Pull the pan off the heat.

Quickly toss the rocket and asparagus with some of the dressing. Arrange the chargrilled peaches on top and drape with wisps of lardo – the lardo should melt a little from the heat of the peaches. Drizzle a little more dressing over the salad, then serve immediately.

I know some people shy away from eating zucchini raw, but this light and refreshing salad might turn that view around. The zucchini aren't cooked but softened in a simple marinade, which also imbues them with fresh, lemony flavours. It's a perfect salad for the height of summer, when zucchini are abundant and at their best (and slaving over a hot stove is a very low priority).

Shaved zucchini with lemon herb dressing and walnuts

Serves 4 as a side

750 g (1 lb 10 oz) green and yellow zucchini (courgettes)
100 ml (3½ fl oz) extra virgin olive oil
finely grated zest and juice of 1 lemon, or to taste
½ garlic clove, grated
sea salt flakes
freshly ground black pepper
1 handful dill, very finely chopped
1 handful mint leaves, very finely chopped
45 g (1½ oz/⅓ cup) walnuts, lightly toasted and chopped
zucchini flowers, to serve (optional)

Using a vegetable peeler, thinly slice the zucchini into ribbons and put in a mixing bowl.

Whisk together the olive oil, lemon zest, lemon juice, garlic, sea salt and black pepper. Pour over the zucchini and toss with your hands. Set aside to marinate for several hours.

Fold the herbs and walnuts through the zucchini, strew with the zucchini flowers (if using) and serve immediately.

Nuts

Filling, delicious and endlessly useful in the kitchen, nuts are also nutritional powerhouses. And yet so many of us forget to include them in our everyday dishes. Step forward Mediterranean cooking to show how it's done.

According to Mediterranean cookery expert Claudia Roden, the Persians, Arabs and Ottomans used nuts to thicken sauces and decorate dishes, and to fill and bedeck pastries. They introduced these techniques throughout the Mediterranean, where they're now used whole, ground, chopped, pounded, raw and roasted in an infinite range of delicious ways.

Creamy, mild and protein-rich, almonds rank among my favourite nuts. The ancient Romans loved them too, giving them to newlyweds as a fertility symbol. I like to thicken sauces by adding a sprinkling of fragrant ground almonds instead of flour. In the Mediterranean they're often served in their shells, a bit like pistachios, as something to nibble on with aperitifs. At home, I tend to toast them, perhaps tossed in olive oil and spices, and serve with a glass of something cold.

Walnuts are also versatile. I often toss a small clutch into cake batter or bread dough – pecans or hazelnuts are good here, too – to add wonderful depth of flavour and texture. They're also fabulous pounded into a chunky sauce along with garlic, herbs and the best extra virgin olive oil. Pistachios are probably the most beguiling nuts. I can't help scattering them over poached fruit, salads, grains, fruit and cakes as much for their photogenic green tinge as their flavour.

Your dish will almost always taste better if you toast nuts before you use them in cooking – this coaxes out the oils, which is where all the flavour hides. Spread the nuts in a single layer on a baking tray and roast for 5 to 10 minutes at 175°C (345°F), shaking the tray now and then to ensure they cook evenly. Watch them like a hawk, as they burn easily – they're ready when they've turned a shade darker and smell toasty.

I am always amazed by the incredible flavour that results from combining these very simple ingredients in a bowl. I don't think there's any finer soup to sip on a hot summer's day.

Cooling tomato, almond and mint soup

Serves 4

120 g (4¼ oz) stale bread, torn
   into pieces
3 tablespoons extra virgin olive
   oil, plus extra for drizzling
1.5 kg (3 lb 5 oz) ripe red
   tomatoes, chopped
3 garlic cloves, chopped
60 g (2¼ oz/⅓ cup) blanched
   almonds
1 teaspoon sea salt flakes,
   or to taste
2 mint leaves, or to taste,
   plus extra shredded leaves
   to serve
thinly sliced jamon, to serve
   (optional)

Put the bread in a bowl and pour 1 tablespoon of the olive oil over it. Set to one side.

Now, place the tomatoes, garlic and almonds in a food processor or blender and blitz until the mixture is as smooth as you can get it. Tip into a sieve set over a bowl and push the solids with the back of a spoon to extract as much liquid as possible. Don't forget to scrape the bottom of the sieve and add these bits to the bowl too. Discard the solids left in the sieve, and pour the liquid back into the blender.

Add the soaked bread, the remaining 2 tablespoons olive oil, the sea salt flakes and mint to the blender, and blitz until smooth. Add a little water if it is too thick. Taste and add more salt or mint if needed – there should just be a fresh back note of mint, so don't overdo it. Chill well, ideally for a couple of hours if you have time.

Serve the soup with mint leaves and jamon (if using) sprinkled on top, and a drizzle of extra virgin olive oil.

This is a comforting and filling soup, but somehow light and refreshing at the same time. I think it has much to do with the pomegranate seeds. I love the cool pop of the slightly tart pomegranate juice when you bite down on the seeds.

Warming wheat grain and pomegranate seed soup

Serves 4

2 tablespoons olive oil
1 onion, chopped
1 carrot, finely chopped
1 celery stalk, chopped
2 teaspoons finely chopped
    rosemary leaves
2 garlic cloves, finely chopped
1 tablespoon tomato paste
    (concentrated purée)
2 tomatoes, chopped
1.5 litres (52 fl oz/6 cups)
    vegetable stock
100 g (3½ oz) wheat grain
sea salt flakes
freshly ground black pepper
100 g (3½ oz) cooked black-
    eyed peas
1 tablespoon red wine vinegar
3 tablespoons pomegranate
    seeds

Warm the olive oil in a saucepan and fry the onion, carrot, celery and rosemary until soft, about 8 minutes. Stir in the garlic and tomato paste, and cook for a few minutes more.

Add the chopped tomatoes, stock and wheat grain to the pan, and season with sea salt and black pepper. Gently simmer for about 1 hour or until the wheat grain is tender – it will retain some bite.

Add the black-eyed peas to the pan and cook for 10 minutes or until warmed through. Pull the pan off the heat, stir in the vinegar and taste for seasoning, adding more salt and pepper if you think it needs it. You should taste just a little sharpness from the vinegar.

Ladle the hot soup into four bowls and serve sprinkled with the pomegranate seeds.

Pop pungent raw garlic into a hot oven, go about your business, then return to find it soft, caramelised and mellow in flavour. For my money, it's one of cooking's magical transformations and used to great effect in this tasty soup. Use young, fresh garlic if you can and roast extra if you like – the pounded roasted cloves are fantastic to have on hand to stir into stews or pasta, or spread on toast, if you're as much of a garlic head as I am.

Garlic and yoghurt soup

Serves 4

3 garlic bulbs, sliced in half
   horizontally
2 tablespoons olive oil
1 litre (35 fl oz/4 cups) good-
   quality chicken or vegetable
   stock
100 g (3½ oz) full-fat Greek-
   style yoghurt
2 eggs, lightly beaten
sea salt flakes
freshly ground black pepper
a squeeze of lemon juice,
   or to taste
4 slices good-quality country-
   style bread, toasted
extra virgin olive oil, for drizzling
60 g (2¼ oz) parmesan cheese,
   grated

Preheat the oven to 200°C (400°F). Remove any papery outer skin from the garlic and place the bulbs in a single layer on a large piece of foil. Drizzle with the 2 tablespoons olive oil, wrap up and bake for 45 minutes or until the cloves are meltingly soft and caramelised. When cool enough to handle, squeeze the garlic flesh into a mortar and pound to a paste.

Bring the stock to a gentle simmer in a large saucepan, then whisk in the garlic paste – I don't mind a few stray bits of garlic but if this troubles you, pour the mixture through a sieve, push through any clumps of garlic, then return the soup to the pan off the heat.

Whisk in the yoghurt and eggs, then return the pan to low heat and stir for a few minutes until the mixture heats through and thickens slightly. Add some sea salt, black pepper and a squeeze of lemon juice, and cook for 1 minute more. Have a taste and add more salt, pepper or lemon juice, if necessary.

Ladle the soup into bowls and add a slice of the toasted bread to each. Drizzle with extra virgin olive oil and sprinkle with the grated parmesan. Serve immediately.

Parsley normally gets stuck in the culinary chorus rather than placed centrestage, but this dish might change your mind about such conventional casting. I admit this soup was a bit of a revelation when I first made it. I love the verdant green colour and the rich woody flavour. It's perfectly lovely without the lemon sprinkle, but if you have time I urge you to go the extra mile and make it – the additional flavours and texture are worth the very small effort.

Parsley soup with walnut and lemon sprinkle

Serves 4

2 tablespoons olive oil
1 large onion, chopped
sea salt flakes
600 g (1 lb 5 oz) potatoes, peeled and cut into 2 cm (¾ inch) cubes
2 garlic cloves, sliced
1 litre (35 fl oz/4 cups) light chicken stock
200 g (7 oz) parsley leaves (fine stalks are OK but discard the thick ones)
lemon juice, to taste
freshly ground black pepper
Greek-style yoghurt, to serve

For the lemon sprinkle

2 tablespoons olive oil
4 tablespoons coarse breadcrumbs, ideally from a crusty loaf
2 tablespoons walnuts, finely chopped
1 garlic clove, finely chopped
grated zest of ½ lemon
2 tablespoons chopped mint leaves
sea salt flakes
freshly ground black pepper

Heat the olive oil in a saucepan over medium–low heat and gently fry the onion with a pinch of sea salt until soft and lightly coloured, about 10 minutes. Add the potatoes and garlic, stir to coat in the oil and cook for a few minutes more, stirring often to prevent sticking. Add the stock and bring to the boil, then reduce the heat to low and cover. Cook for 10 minutes or until the potatoes are tender, then set aside to cool a little.

While the potatoes are cooking, make the lemon sprinkle. Heat the olive oil in a frying pan over medium–high heat, add the breadcrumbs and walnuts, then stir-fry until the breadcrumbs are starting to turn golden. Add the garlic and cook for a few minutes more. Remove the pan from the heat and stir in the lemon zest, mint, and sea salt and black pepper to taste. Set to one side.

Now, bring a large saucepan of water to the boil and fill a bowl with iced water. Blanch the parsley for 20 seconds, then drain, reserving the cooking liquid. Plunge the parsley into the iced water (this will stop the cooking and preserve the colour), then drain. Squeeze out any excess water into the reserved cooking liquid, and roughly chop.

Transfer the potatoes and stock to a food processor; add the parsley and blitz until smooth. You'll still have some flecks of parsley, but that's fine. Return the soup to the pan and set over low heat to warm through – try not to heat it for too long or the parsley loses some of its fresh colour. Add a little reserved parsley liquid if you like a thinner soup.

Add a splash of lemon juice to the parsley soup, then stir and have a taste – add more lemon juice or sea salt and black pepper until it's just the way you like it. Ladle the soup into bowls and serve topped with a swirl of yoghurt and the lemon sprinkle.

Thick, nourishing and full of comforting flavours, I crave this famous Greek soup during winter. The garnish is almost as important as the soup in my opinion – the capers provide a sharp and refreshing contrast to the soothing richness of the split peas. If you prefer to enjoy this as a thicker dip or side dish – almost like a dal without the Indian flavours – just cook the split peas with a little less liquid, and for a little longer.

Yellow split pea soup with red onions and capers

Serves 4

90 ml (3 fl oz) olive oil
1 white onion, finely chopped
sea salt flakes
1 teaspoon ground cumin
200 g (7 oz) yellow split peas
1 litre (35 fl oz/4 cups) chicken or vegetable stock
1 garlic clove, bruised with the side of a knife
2 tablespoons lemon juice, or to taste
freshly ground black pepper

For the garnish

2 tablespoons olive oil
1 large red onion, halved and sliced
a pinch of sea salt flakes
1 teaspoon ground coriander
2 tablespoons capers, rinsed and chopped
2 tablespoons finely chopped flat-leaf parsley leaves

Heat 2 tablespoons of the olive oil in a saucepan and fry the white onion with a pinch of sea salt until soft, about 8 minutes. Stir in the ground cumin and cook for a few minutes more. Add the split peas, stock and garlic, and bring to the boil, skimming off any scum that rises to the top. Reduce the heat and simmer for around 1 hour, stirring now and then. The split peas should be collapsing and the liquid almost absorbed; add more water if they look like drying out.

Pour off and reserve any liquid left in the split peas, then transfer the mixture to a food processor along with the cooked garlic clove. Add the remaining olive oil and the lemon juice, and season with sea salt and black pepper. Pulse to the desired consistency, adding a little of the reserved cooking liquid to loosen if needed.

While the split peas are simmering, prepare the garnish. Heat the olive oil in a frying pan, add the red onion and sea salt, and cook over low heat until caramelised, about 15 minutes. Stir in the coriander and cook for 1 minute more.

To serve, ladle the soup into bowls and top with the onion mixture, capers and parsley.

This cold soup is vibrant, silky and refreshing, and a brilliant way to eat one of the most nutritious vegetables on the planet. There's virtually no cooking involved, just blanching the watercress and broad beans. The quick plunge into boiling water mellows some of the peppery flavour of the watercress, and even friends who aren't normally partial to watercress love this soup.

Watercress and yoghurt soup with broad beans

Serves 4

400 g (14 oz) tender watercress leaves (thin stalks are fine but discard thick ones), plus extra to serve

400 g (14 oz) Greek-style yoghurt, plus extra to serve

3 tablespoons lemon juice, or to taste

16 basil leaves

250 ml (9 fl oz/1 cup) milk

3 tablespoons extra virgin olive oil, plus extra for drizzling

125 ml (4 fl oz/½ cup) cold chicken or vegetable stock, plus extra if needed

sea salt flakes

freshly ground black pepper

120 g (4¼ oz) podded broad beans

3 teaspoons nigella seeds

Blanch the watercress in boiling water for just a few seconds, then drain, refresh in cold water and squeeze out as much water as you can. Pop the watercress in a blender with the remaining ingredients except the broad beans and nigella seeds. Blitz until smooth and creamy, adding more stock if needed for the desired consistency. Have a taste and add some more salt and pepper or lemon juice if needed. Chill.

Cook the broad beans in boiling salted water for 1 minute or until just tender. Drain, refresh in cold water and slip the beans from their skins.

Ladle the soup into bowls and top with a spoonful of yoghurt, the broad beans and extra watercress, and a sprinkle of nigella seeds. Drizzle with a little extra virgin olive oil before serving.

Hearty and warming, with some spicy crunch from the chickpea croutons, this is a yummy and satisfying winter soup that everyone seems to love. The tahini adds a nutty creaminess and just a hint of sesame.

Cannellini bean and tahini soup with spiced chickpea croutons

Serves 4

2 tablespoons olive oil
1 small onion, chopped
1 carrot, chopped
1 celery stalk, chopped
sea salt flakes
2 garlic cloves
1 teaspoon ras el hanout
750 ml (26 fl oz/3 cups) chicken or vegetable stock
500 g (1 lb 2 oz) cooked or tinned cannellini beans, rinsed and drained
1 teaspoon chopped thyme leaves, plus extra sprigs to serve
1½ tablespoons tahini
lemon juice, to taste
freshly ground black pepper

For the spiced chickpeas

120 g (4¼ oz) cooked or tinned chickpeas, rinsed and drained
2 tablespoons olive oil
½ teaspoon cayenne pepper
½ teaspoon smoked paprika
sea salt flakes
freshly ground black pepper

Heat the olive oil in a saucepan, add the onion, carrot, celery and a pinch of sea salt, and gently fry over medium heat, stirring frequently, for about 8 minutes or until soft. Add the garlic and ras el hanout, and fry for a further 2 minutes. Pour in the stock, add the cannellini beans and thyme, then gently simmer for 10 minutes.

While the soup is cooking, make the spiced chickpeas. Using paper towel, dry the chickpeas and gently rub them to remove the skins (be careful, as you don't want to squash them). Heat the olive oil in a frying pan and fry the chickpeas over medium heat for 10 minutes or until crisp and golden – take care, as they splatter a bit. Transfer to paper towel to soak up the excess oil, then place in a bowl and toss with the spices, sea salt and black pepper. Set aside.

When the soup is cooked, set aside to cool a little, then carefully ladle into a blender, add the tahini and blitz until smooth, or use a stick blender. (A food processor also works well, but your soup will retain a little texture from the bean skins.)

Return the soup to the pan and warm through over medium heat. Stir in a little lemon juice, then taste and add a little sea salt, black pepper or more lemon juice if needed.

Ladle the soup into bowls and serve with the spiced chickpeas and thyme sprigs on top.

Meat, poultry & fish

This recipe is inspired by a fond memory from my distant backpacking days: watching the sunset from a cliff top on the Greek island of Santorini, while devouring the most delicious souvlaki I had ever eaten. Marinating the lamb in yoghurt is not strictly traditional, but it helps tenderise the meat and really carries the flavour of the spices. Try to accompany this with the Pillowy pitta bread from page 20. It's also lovely with the Chunky fennel and radish tzatziki (page 42).

Yoghurt-marinated lamb with charred tomato relish in flatbread

Serves 4

600 g (1 lb 5 oz) lamb neck fillet
120 g (4¼ oz) Greek-style
  yoghurt
grated zest and juice of 1 lemon,
  plus lemon wedges to serve
3 garlic cloves, crushed
2 tablespoons olive oil
1½ teaspoons smoked paprika
1½ teaspoons ground cumin
1½ teaspoons dried oregano
sea salt flakes
freshly ground black pepper
warm flatbreads, to serve
mixed salad leaves, to serve
1 large handful mixed herbs
  such as mint, flat-leaf parsley
  and coriander (cilantro) leaves

For the tomato relish

2 large ripe tomatoes
½ garlic clove
2 tablespoons extra virgin olive
  oil, or to taste
1 tablespoon sherry vinegar,
  or to taste
a pinch of Aleppo pepper or
  cayenne pepper
½ teaspoon honey
sea salt flakes
freshly ground black pepper

First, cut the lamb into 3 cm (1¼ inch) cubes. In a large shallow ceramic or glass bowl, stir together the yoghurt, lemon zest, lemon juice, garlic, 1 tablespoon of the olive oil, the spices, sea salt and black pepper. Add the lamb and mix with your hands to coat, then cover with plastic wrap and transfer to the fridge to marinate for at least a couple of hours.

While the lamb is marinating, make the tomato relish. Preheat your grill (broiler) to high and line the grill tray with foil. Cook the tomatoes as close to the element as you can, turning them now and then, until they are blackened and blistered all over. Transfer the tomatoes and juices to a food processor. Add the garlic, olive oil, sherry vinegar, Aleppo or cayenne pepper, honey, sea salt and black pepper. Blitz until you have a slightly chunky sauce. Have a taste and add some more salt, pepper, oil or vinegar if needed. Set aside until needed.

About 30 minutes before you are ready to cook the lamb, remove it from the fridge to return to room temperature. Heat a frying pan or chargrill pan until very hot and add the remaining 1 tablespoon olive oil. Add the lamb to the pan, scraping off the excess marinade, and fry, shaking the pan frequently, for 5 minutes or until charred on the outside and done to your liking on the inside.

Stuff the warm flatbreads with the lamb, salad leaves, herbs and tomato relish and serve with lemon wedges.

Sticky chicken is full of flavour and universally popular. I love bringing the pan to the table to serve so everyone can see and smell how burnished and sticky the chicken looks straight from the oven. Don't panic if you can't lay your hands on ouzo or pastis, just use white wine. Make sure you use the smaller, more tender Greek olives rather than the enormous meaty Spanish ones that don't cook down quite so nicely.

Sticky chicken with ouzo, olives and charred lemons

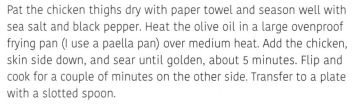

Serves 4

8 chicken thighs, bone in,
   skin on
sea salt flakes
freshly ground black pepper
2 tablespoons olive oil
1 lemon, cut into 8 wedges
2 garlic bulbs, cloves separated
   and peeled
4 white onions, sliced
1 tablespoon za'atar
3 teaspoons dried oregano
1 teaspoon fennel seeds
3 tablespoons ouzo, pastis or
   other anise-flavoured liqueur
150 g (5½ oz) pitted green
   Greek olives
juice of 2 lemons

Pat the chicken thighs dry with paper towel and season well with sea salt and black pepper. Heat the olive oil in a large ovenproof frying pan (I use a paella pan) over medium heat. Add the chicken, skin side down, and sear until golden, about 5 minutes. Flip and cook for a couple of minutes on the other side. Transfer to a plate with a slotted spoon.

Pour all the oil out of the pan and then pour 2 tablespoons back in, keeping the rest to use later. Add the lemon wedges and garlic, and fry until the lemon wedges are charred on both sides. Transfer the lemon and garlic to the plate with the chicken.

Preheat the oven to 180°C (350°F).

Add the onions, za'atar, oregano, fennel seeds and a pinch of sea salt to the frying pan, and stir to coat in the oil. Gently fry over medium–low heat, stirring frequently, for 10 minutes or until the onions are soft, sweet and golden. Add more oil if they start to stick to the pan or colour too quickly. Pour in the alcohol and stir with a wooden spoon as it bubbles up to scrape up all the delicious bits stuck to the pan. Cook until the smell of the alcohol subsides.

Arrange the chicken in the pan in a single layer, skin side up, then nestle the olives, lemon wedges and garlic in between. Pour the lemon juice over the top and add a little more salt and pepper.

Roast for 45 minutes or until the chicken skin is crisp and golden, and the flesh is very tender. This dish is delicious served with rice or other grains, with the pan juices spooned over the top.

Lamb and orange is a classic partnership in French cooking, and this stew is luscious, hearty, healthy and tasty. It requires a bit of advance preparation by way of soaking the beans overnight: I find remembering to do this is the trickiest part of this recipe. The time it takes to cook dried beans varies widely depending on their age – anything from 45 minutes to a couple of hours if the beans are quite old. Dried beans are firmer, creamier and more flavourful, but you can use tinned if necessary. You will need 400 g (14 oz) tinned beans (drained weight), but add them at the end with the cavolo nero.

Lamb, orange and white bean stew

Serves 4

250 g (9 oz) dried gigantes beans or large butterbeans
1 tablespoon ground coriander
2 fat garlic cloves, roughly chopped
finely grated zest and juice of 2 oranges
100 ml (3½ fl oz) olive oil
sea salt flakes
2 x lamb neck fillets, about 300 g (10½ oz) each, cut into 3 cm (1¼ inch) cubes
1 onion, chopped
1 carrot, chopped
½ fennel bulb, chopped
1 heaped teaspoon dried rosemary
1 tablespoon tomato paste (concentrated purée)
125 ml (4 fl oz/½ cup) red wine
2 tomatoes, chopped
250 ml (9 fl oz/1 cup) lamb or vegetable stock
freshly ground black pepper
3 bay leaves
100 g (3½ oz) cavolo nero (Tuscan kale) or other kale, thinly sliced
crusty bread, to serve

Begin the night before you want to eat by soaking the beans in plenty of cold water. The next day, rinse well, place in a saucepan and cover with cold water. Simmer until the beans are just tender, then drain and set aside.

While the beans are cooking, marinate the lamb. Put the coriander in a mortar; add the garlic, orange zest, 30 ml (1 fl oz) of the olive oil and a generous pinch of sea salt, and pound to a paste. Put the lamb in a shallow bowl, add the paste and massage into the meat with your hands. Put to one side until the beans are done.

Heat 30 ml (1 fl oz) of the olive oil in a saucepan and brown the lamb on all sides – you will need to do this in batches so the meat doesn't steam. Transfer to a plate with a slotted spoon as you go.

Wipe out the pan, add the remaining 2 tablespoons olive oil and fry the onion, carrot and fennel with the rosemary and a pinch of salt until the vegetables are very soft, about 8 minutes. Stir in the tomato paste. Cook, stirring, for a few minutes more until it smells fragrant.

Return the lamb to the pan and stir to combine with the vegetables. Increase the heat, add the wine and let it bubble up and then reduce. Add the drained beans to the pan along with the tomatoes, orange juice, stock and enough boiling water to just cover the meat. Season generously with sea salt and black pepper, tuck in the bay leaves and reduce the heat. Simmer very gently for 1 hour and 50 minutes – the meat should be meltingly tender by this point.

Add the sliced cavolo nero, pushing it under the liquid, and cook for 10 minutes more.

Serve the stew with some crusty bread to mop up the juices.

Goat meat has long been standard fare across the Mediterranean but it used to be difficult to find elsewhere. In the UK and Australia we have finally realised it's not only delicious but also healthy, being relatively lean and loaded with potassium and iron. If you're new to goat, this rustic dish will win you over, but one tip: choose a shoulder with plenty of fat, as it can dry out during cooking.

Falling-apart, milk-roasted goat

Serves 8 generously

500 ml (17 fl oz/2 cups) goat's milk

4 garlic cloves, bruised with the side of a knife

3 bay leaves

½ cinnamon stick

3 x 4 cm (1½ inch) strips lemon zest

3 tablespoons olive oil, plus extra if needed

2 kg (4 lb 8 oz) shoulder of goat, bone in

3 large onions, sliced

3 carrots, roughly chopped

sea salt flakes

1 handful thyme sprigs

juice of ½ lemon, or to taste

freshly ground black pepper

2 teaspoons cornflour (cornstarch), if needed

Pour the milk into a saucepan, add the garlic, bay leaves, cinnamon stick and lemon zest, and bring to a simmer. Remove the pan from the heat and set aside for the flavours to develop.

Preheat the oven to 140°C (275°F). Heat 2 tablespoons of the olive oil in a heavy roasting tin large enough to hold the goat shoulder easily, then brown all over on medium–high heat – it's an awkward shape, I know, but do what you can to get some colour all over. Transfer the shoulder to a plate. Add a splash more olive oil if there's none left in the tin – or spoon off all but 2 tablespoons if there's plenty – and add the onions and carrots. Fry over medium heat with a pinch of sea salt until the vegetables have softened and started to take on some colour. Remove from the heat and pop the goat shoulder on top of the vegetables, skin side up. Pour the milk mixture over the goat. Arrange the thyme sprigs around the meat, squeeze the lemon half over the goat and generously season with sea salt and black pepper.

Cover the goat with a double layer of foil and roast for 3 hours. Remove the foil, baste the goat with the milk, then increase the oven to 180°C (350°F). Roast, uncovered, for a further 1 hour, basting with the milk now and then, until the meat is meltingly tender and almost falling off the bone. Transfer the goat to a plate, loosely cover with foil and leave to rest for at least 15 minutes.

Meanwhile, pour the milky mixture from the tin through a sieve into a saucepan (it might look a bit odd, with lots of curd visible). Push down on the vegetables in the sieve with the back of a spoon to extract as much of the juice as possible. Simmer over medium–high heat, stirring, until reduced a little. Remove from the heat, stir in lemon juice to taste and check for seasoning. The slightly curdled appearance of the sauce doesn't bother me, but if you're troubled, scoop 125 ml (4 fl oz/½ cup) of the sauce into a bowl, whisk in the cornflour until smooth, then return this mixture to the pan. Stir over medium heat until thickened.

Use forks to shred the goat meat. Serve with the sauce alongside.

Not so long ago, the plight of veal calves reared and transported in cramped crates quite rightly deterred many people from eating veal in the UK. But things have changed. High-welfare veal, known as rose or pink veal, is now produced from male dairy calves that would otherwise be shot soon after birth as a waste product. Rose veal is delicious, but choose your supplier carefully.

Eggplants stuffed with rose veal, fennel and ricotta

Serves 4

2 large eggplants (aubergines), about 500 g (1 lb 2 oz) each
3 tablespoons olive oil
sea salt flakes
freshly ground black pepper
2 teaspoons fennel seeds
½ fennel bulb, chopped
1 carrot, diced
1 onion, chopped
½ teaspoon ground cinnamon
½ teaspoon smoked paprika
1 garlic clove, finely chopped
1 tablespoon tomato paste (concentrated purée)
500 g (1 lb 2 oz) minced (ground) high-welfare veal
4 tablespoons pine nuts
3 tablespoons tomato passata
lemon juice, to taste
100 g (3½ oz) ricotta cheese
60 g (2¼ oz) parmesan cheese, grated

Preheat the oven to 200°C (400°F) and lightly oil a roasting tin. Slice the eggplants in half lengthways and drizzle 2 teaspoons of the olive oil over each half. Season generously with sea salt and black pepper, and roast for 30–40 minutes or until the flesh is very tender. Set aside to cool a little, then scoop out the flesh, leaving a little next to the skin. Leave the shells in the tin. Chop the flesh and set aside.

While the eggplants are roasting, toast the fennel seeds in a large dry frying pan until aromatic and lightly coloured. Tip into a bowl and set to one side.

Heat the remaining olive oil in the same frying pan, add the chopped fennel, carrot, onion, cinnamon, paprika and a pinch of sea salt, and gently fry over medium heat until very soft, about 8 minutes. Add the garlic and tomato paste, and fry for 2 minutes more. Add the veal, pine nuts and toasted fennel seeds, increase the heat and break up the meat with the side of a spoon so there are no clumps. Cook for 1–2 minutes, without stirring, so the meat develops a bit of a crust on the bottom, then stir and repeat until all the meat is coloured and the pan is quite dry. Pour in the passata and stir, scraping the pan with a wooden spoon to loosen any caramelised bits. Simmer for a few minutes until the meat is cooked through and coated in just a little sauce – add a splash of water if it's drying out, but you don't want much liquid at all.

Pull the pan off the heat and stir in the reserved eggplant flesh and a splash of lemon juice, then fold in spoonfuls of the ricotta, bit by bit. It's good to have small pieces of ricotta that aren't completely amalgamated. Have a taste and add more salt, pepper or lemon juice if needed.

Spoon the mixture into the eggplant shells. Sprinkle the parmesan on top and roast for about 10 minutes or until the cheese is bubbling. Leave to cool for a couple of minutes before serving each person an eggplant half, ideally with a crisp green salad.

This dish exemplifies the best of Mediterranean cooking: a simple and delicious dish that can be served at the table straight from the roasting tin. The aim is to have all the juices from the chicken drip down over the potatoes as they roast. You could ask your butcher to butterfly the chicken, but I find this simple task very pleasing.

Roast butterflied chicken with herbs and potatoes

Serves 4–6

1 large free-range chicken,
    about 2 kg (4 lb 8 oz)
700 g (1 lb 9 oz) potatoes,
    peeled and chopped

For the marinade

125 ml (4 fl oz/½ cup) extra
    virgin olive oil
2 tablespoons warm water
finely grated zest and juice
    of 1 lemon
5 garlic cloves, crushed
1½ tablespoons dried oregano
1 tablespoon lemon verbena
    or lemon thyme leaves
a generous pinch of saffron,
    chopped
1 teaspoon sea salt flakes
freshly ground black pepper

Put all the marinade ingredients in a small bowl. Stir to combine, then set to one side.

Now, butterfly the chicken. Place the chicken on a chopping board, breast side down, with the legs towards you. Using sharp kitchen scissors, cut along each side of the parson's nose, through the rib cage to the other end of the bird to remove the backbone. (Don't throw the backbone away: reserve it for stock or freeze it until you're ready to use it.) Turn the chicken over and press down with the heel of your hand to flatten it.

Put the chicken in a non-metallic shallow bowl large enough for the bird to lay flat, pour over three-quarters of the marinade and massage all over. Turn the bird so the skin is on the bottom, cover with plastic wrap and chill in the fridge for at least an hour or ideally overnight.

Preheat the oven to 200°C (400°F) and have two oven racks ready: one for the potatoes and another for the chicken.

Put the potatoes in a roasting tin. Pour in the remaining marinade, toss to coat and place on the lower oven rack. Shake any excess marinade off the chicken and place the bird directly on the top oven rack, skin side up. Arrange the racks so that the chicken sits directly above and as close as possible to the tray of potatoes to catch the juices. Bake for 45 minutes or until the chicken juices run clear when you pierce the flesh with a knife between the thigh and the breast.

Serve the chicken with the potatoes, with some of the lemony pan juices spooned over each serving.

I love pork chops. Apart from the marinating time (which could be reduced if you're in a hurry), this is a quick and tasty meal, and a little bit special too. The slightly sharp, spicy notes of the juniper work wonderfully with the fennel and the pork. Make sure the chops are nice and thick so they don't dry out. Cannellini beans tossed with a vinaigrette make a lovely accompaniment.

Juicy pork chops with rosemary, juniper and braised fennel

Serves 4

4 thick boneless pork loin
   chops
30 ml (1 fl oz) olive oil
2 large fennel bulbs, trimmed
   and cut into eight pieces
   lengthways
a splash of ouzo or pastis
   (white wine works fine)
125 ml (4 fl oz/½ cup) chicken
   stock
juice of ½ lemon

For the marinade

12 juniper berries
4 garlic cloves
2 tablespoons roughly chopped
   rosemary leaves
finely grated zest and juice
   of 1 lemon
1 teaspoon sea salt flakes
freshly ground black pepper
30 ml (1 fl oz) olive oil

First, make your marinade. Pop the juniper berries into a frying pan and cook, shaking frequently, until they smell gorgeous. Tip into a mortar, add the garlic, rosemary, lemon zest, sea salt and black pepper, and pound to a rough paste. Add the lemon juice and olive oil, then stir to make a lovely aromatic slurry.

Put the pork chops in a large shallow glass or ceramic bowl, pour the marinade over them and rub in well. Cover with plastic wrap and transfer to the fridge for a couple of hours. About 30 minutes before you are ready to cook the pork chops, take them out of the fridge to return to room temperature and preheat the oven to 220°C (425°F).

Now, get on with the fennel. Heat 3 teaspoons of the olive oil in a frying pan and add the fennel pieces in a single layer. Fry over medium heat, turning now and then, until they are starting to turn golden all over. Increase the heat to high, add the alcohol and let it bubble up for a few moments, shaking the pan. Reduce the heat to low, add the stock, cover with a lid or baking tray and gently cook for 15 minutes. Uncover, increase the heat and fry for 5 minutes or until the liquid has almost completely evaporated. The fennel should be very tender and nearly caramelised. Set aside to keep warm.

Now, cook the pork chops. Heat the remaining oil in an ovenproof frying pan until very hot. Scrape the marinade off the chops, then quickly sear them on both sides until they take on some colour, about 2–3 minutes in total. Carefully transfer the pan to the oven and cook for 5–10 minutes or until the pork is just cooked through. Transfer to a plate and loosely cover with foil.

Set the pan over medium–high heat, add the lemon juice and stir to scrape up all the goodness from the base to make your sauce.

Serve the pork chops on the fennel with the sauce poured over.

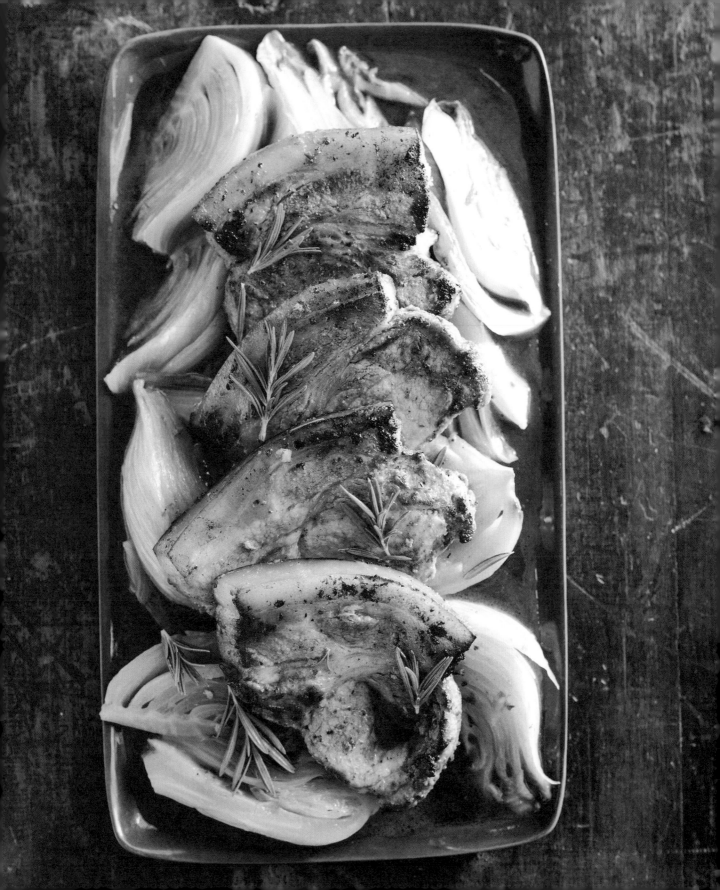

Mouth-puckering pickled fruit and vegetables are enjoyed across the Mediterranean and I love them. They are a great way to store excess produce in times of plenty. I also love pickles as a foil to oily fish, cooked and cold meat, as well as cheese. Turnips, cauliflower, carrots and, of course, cucumbers are commonly pickled in the Mediterranean, as well as a wide variety of fruit. Here I've assembled a quick pickle made with rhubarb and radishes that's very pretty and makes your mouth tingle.

Soused sardines on toast with pickled rhubarb salad

Serves 4

75 g (2½ oz) radishes
½ fennel bulb
75 g (2½ oz) trimmed rhubarb
8 sardine fillets
½ teaspoon fine sea salt
8 slices country-style bread
olive oil, for brushing
baby salad leaves, to serve

For the quick pickle liquid

90 ml (3 fl oz) white balsamic
    vinegar
40 g (1½ oz) caster (superfine)
    sugar
½ teaspoon fine sea salt
½ teaspoon coriander seeds
4 pink peppercorns
½ star anise
1 bay leaf

First, make the pickle liquid. Pop all the ingredients into a small saucepan with 4 tablespoons water and simmer over medium heat until the sugar has dissolved. Set aside for 10 minutes, then strain to remove the aromatic bits and bobs.

Very thinly slice the radishes and fennel, ideally on a mandolin. Cut the rhubarb into short lengths and then into very thin slices. Put all the vegetables in a bowl and pour over the strained pickle liquid. Set aside for 20 minutes.

Pat the sardines dry with paper towel, sprinkle both sides with the salt, and set aside for 20 minutes. Preheat the grill (broiler) to high and line the grill rack with foil.

Arrange the sardines on the grill tray, skin side up, and cook for 2 minutes or until they are bubbling and starting to turn golden. Depending on thickness, the sardines might be cooked through at this point. If not, flip them and cook for 1 minute more. Place the sardines in a single layer in a wide shallow bowl. Drain the pickled vegetables, reserving the pickling liquid, then pour the liquid over the sardines. Set aside for 10 minutes.

While this is happening, brush the bread with olive oil and lightly toast in a chargrill pan or under the grill.

Remove the sardines from the pickling liquid and serve them on the toasted bread with the pickled vegetables on top and salad leaves on the side.

This deeply flavoured dish – my take on a traditional Provençal bourride – is a little bit indulgent but makes seafood lovers swoon. I choose monkfish for its sweetness and firm texture but it can be pricey and is only available in the Northern Hemisphere, so feel free to replace it with thick fillets of other meaty white fish such as sea bass, halibut or snapper.

Fisherman's stew with saffron aïoli

Serves 4

500 g (1 lb 2 oz) monkfish fillets (see note above)
2 tablespoons olive oil
½ fennel bulb, about 150 g (5½ oz), very thinly sliced
½ large onion, cut into wedges
1 carrot, chopped
1 garlic clove, finely chopped
sea salt flakes
250 ml (9 fl oz/1 cup) dry white wine
2 pieces of orange zest, each about 5 cm (2 inches) long
2 bay leaves
1 litre (35 fl oz/4 cups) best-quality fish stock
8 raw large prawns (shrimp) with shells
freshly ground black pepper
4 smallish pieces toasted country-style bread or Olive oil bread (page 19)
finely chopped flat-leaf parsley leaves, to serve

For the saffron aïoli

1 egg yolk
2 large garlic cloves, crushed
1 tablespoon lemon juice
a generous pinch of saffron threads, chopped
a pinch of sea salt flakes
125 ml (4 fl oz/½ cup) olive oil

First, make the aïoli. Put the egg yolk, garlic, lemon juice, saffron and sea salt in a mixing bowl. Sit the bowl on a folded damp tea towel on your work surface to help keep it stable. Using a hand whisk or hand-held electric beaters, beat until well combined. Pour in 1 tablespoon of the olive oil a drop at a time, beating as you go, until the mixture turns pale and starts to thicken. Pour in the remaining olive oil in a very thin stream, beating all the time, until the mixture is very thick and creamy. Put to one side.

Preheat the oven to 100°C (200°F). Remove the skin and membranes from the monkfish fillets and cut them into 7 cm (2¾ inch) pieces.

Warm the olive oil in a large frying pan over medium heat. Gently cook the fennel, onion, carrot, garlic and a pinch of sea salt for a couple of minutes until starting to soften. Increase the heat, then add the wine, orange zest and bay leaves. Gently simmer until the liquid has reduced enough to just cover the base of the pan.

Stir in the stock and bring to the boil, then reduce the heat to a gentle simmer. Add the fish and prawns, and gently cook until the fish is just cooked and the prawns are pink – about 5 minutes. If the prawns are done first, remove them from the pan with a slotted spoon and pop them on a plate, followed by the fish when it's done. Loosely cover with foil and transfer to the oven to keep warm.

Strain the stock, then return it to the pan and boil until reduced by half, skimming off any scum that rises to the top. Reduce the heat to low, then scoop out 125 ml (4 fl oz/½ cup) or so of the stock and pour into the aïoli, stirring well. Pour this mixture back into the pan and whisk until light, creamy and warmed through, but don't let it boil. Season to taste with sea salt and black pepper.

To serve, place a piece of the toasted bread in each of four shallow bowls, arrange the fish and prawns on top and pour the sauce over the top. Scatter with a little parsley and serve immediately.

Seafood

It's logical that fish and shellfish should be key sources of healthy protein in the Mediterranean. Seafood is abundant, varied and eaten supremely fresh, so very little needs to be done to it in terms of cooking. As well as the recipes in this chapter, I love cooking seafood very simply in a chargrill pan or on a barbecue, with nothing more than olive oil, lemon juice and sea salt – or some herbs and sliced citrus tucked into the cavity of whole fish. This is how I do it ...

First, I pat my seafood dry with paper towel, then lightly brush it with a thin slick of olive oil before seasoning generously on both sides with salt and pepper. I find that doing this up to a couple of hours before cooking (I keep it in the fridge, then allow it to return to room temperature first) really enhances the flavour.

Seafood sticks more than meat or chicken, so it's important that the chargrill or barbecue is very clean, very hot and rubbed lightly with oil. The golden rule is to fight the impulse to flip seafood too early or too often, before it develops the lovely caramelised crust that carries loads of flavour and prevents sticking. I cook thinner fish fillets on one side until opaque almost all the way through – skin side down first, if applicable – then flip and cook very briefly (if at all) on the other side. I generally cook thicker fillets or steaks for equal time on both sides. For whole fish, carefully turn the fish when the skin is brown – if the skin on the other side threatens to burn before it is cooked through, just reduce the heat or move it to a cooler part of the barbecue until it's done.

To serve, simply squeeze some lemon juice over the top, add maybe a drizzle of extra virgin olive oil and some sea salt. That's it.

Beautiful mackerel, with its iridescent silver and blue stripes, is abundant in the Mediterranean. But even in countries such as Spain, Greece and Italy, it's not the most popular of fish and I don't know why. Oil-rich and meaty, the flesh is highly nutritious and packed with flavour. It's also cheap and sustainable – so what's not to like? You do have to watch out for bones in mackerel, but you can remove the backbone before roasting. To do this, gently but firmly roll the fish on the work surface to break the backbone, then carefully remove it from the inside by teasing it away from the flesh with your fingers, starting at the head. It takes a bit of practice but works a treat.

Baked mackerel with pine nut stuffing and roast cherry tomatoes

Serves 4

4 whole mackerel, about 300 g (10½ oz) each, gutted and cleaned (see note above about backbone)
4 bunches large cherry tomatoes on the vine
olive oil, for drizzling
sea salt flakes
freshly ground black pepper
rocket (arugula) leaves, to serve

For the stuffing

2 tablespoons olive oil
1 onion, chopped
sea salt flakes
2 garlic cloves, finely chopped
2 tablespoons fresh or dry breadcrumbs
20 g (¾ oz) raisins
30 g (1 oz) pine nuts
a pinch of ground cinnamon
a pinch of ground allspice
1 tablespoon dried marjoram
1 large handful parsley leaves, chopped
finely grated zest of ½ lemon
freshly ground black pepper

Start by preparing the stuffing. Heat the olive oil in a frying pan and fry the onion with a pinch of sea salt until soft and starting to colour, about 8 minutes. Add the chopped garlic and cook for a few minutes more. Toss in the breadcrumbs, raisins, pine nuts, spices and marjoram. Cook, stirring now and then so it doesn't catch, for 5 minutes or until lightly toasted and smelling fragrant. Remove from the heat and stir in the parsley, lemon zest and sea salt and black pepper to taste.

Preheat the oven to 180°C (350°F) and find a roasting tin that will hold the fish and tomatoes snugly. Divide the stuffing equally among the fish cavities and sit them in the roasting tin, stuffing side up (it might take a little arranging to get them to stay upright). Add the tomatoes to the tin, then drizzle everything with olive oil and season with sea salt and black pepper. Roast for about 20 minutes or until the fish is just cooked but still moist and the tomatoes are starting to burst.

Serve each guest a whole fish, a bunch of tomatoes and a handful of rocket.

Nduja is a fiery pork paste from Calabria that's now readily available outside of southern Italy, thankfully. The flavour and spicy kick are quite addictive and elevate a simple dish into something extra tasty. Nduja is a bit of an ugly beast (it comes packed in pork intestine and tied with string) but simply melts into whatever dish you're cooking. It's much easier to use, in fact, than it is to say: *en-doo-ya*.

Sizzling garlic prawns with nduja

**Serves 2–4 as a starter
or tapas**

90 ml (3 fl oz) olive oil
6 garlic cloves, finely chopped
1 large handful flat-leaf parsley
    leaves, about 15 g (½ oz),
    chopped
40–60 g (1½–2¼ oz) nduja,
    cut or torn into small pieces
750 g (1 lb 10 oz) raw medium
    prawns with shells
finely grated zest of ½ lemon
sea salt flakes
crusty bread, to serve

Pour the olive oil into a large frying pan set over medium–low heat. Add the chopped garlic and parsley and stir constantly for a couple of minutes while the garlic and parsley infuse the oil – you don't really want to fry (or burn!) them.

Add the nduja and stir until melted into the oil. Increase the heat to high, add the prawns and cook, stirring, until they have turned pink – 3 minutes should do it.

Sprinkle the lemon zest and some sea salt over the prawns and take the pan to the table for guests to serve themselves, with some crusty bread to mop up the delicious oil.

A favourite dish at our house, and not just because the fried gigantes beans taste like tiny fried potatoes, this is also super speedy to prepare if you keep a stash of cooked white beans in the freezer (see my tips for this on page 136). I implore you not to overcook the tuna – this wonderful fish should be juicy and pink in the middle, not like the sole of your boot.

Tuna with crispy gigantes beans and rocket salsa verde

Serves 4

4 tablespoons olive oil, plus
   extra for brushing
juice of 1 lemon
1 garlic clove, crushed
sea salt flakes
freshly ground black pepper
4 tuna steaks, about 140 g
   (5 oz) each
200 g (7 oz) cooked gigantes
   beans or other cooked or
   tinned large white beans

For the salsa verde

30 g (1 oz) rocket (arugula)
   leaves
30 g (1 oz) parsley leaves
6 anchovy fillets in oil, drained
1 tablespoon capers in brine,
   rinsed and drained
2 tablespoons red wine vinegar,
   or to taste
90 ml (3 fl oz) extra virgin olive
   oil, or to taste

Start by marinating the tuna. Whisk together half the olive oil, the lemon juice, garlic, sea salt and black pepper. Put the tuna in a shallow ceramic or glass bowl, add the marinade and turn to coat. Set aside while you get on with the rest of the dish.

To make the salsa verde, put all the ingredients in a food processor and blitz until smoothish – it's quite nice to have a little texture. Have a taste to see if you like the piquancy and add more oil or vinegar if the flavour needs adjusting. Set aside.

Rinse the beans and pat dry with paper towel. Heat the remaining olive oil in a large frying pan, add the beans in a single layer and cook for a couple of minutes without turning until crisp and golden underneath. Flip and cook until golden and crisp on the other side. Set aside to keep warm.

Heat a chargrill pan until very hot and cook the tuna for 1–2 minutes on each side, depending on the thickness of the fillets, until charred with stripes on the outside but still pink in the middle.

Toss the crispy beans with enough of the salsa verde to coat well and serve with the sliced tuna. Spoon more salsa verde alongside the tuna and put the rest on the table so guests can help themselves to more.

Whenever I get the chance to buy baby octopus, I seize it because this is one my family's favourite meals. A lot of people worry about cooking with octopus for fear it will turn out tough, but that's really not an issue if you tenderise it properly first. In the Mediterranean they often do this by bashing it against a rock. Happily, freezing it first serves the same purpose, so either buy your octopus frozen and thaw it before cooking, or plan ahead and pop fresh octopus in the freezer a day or so before you want to cook it.

Warm baby octopus salad with chorizo and potatoes

Serves 4

700 g (1 lb 9 oz) frozen cleaned baby octopus, thawed
500 ml (17 fl oz/2 cups) vegetable stock
3 lemon slices, plus lemon wedges to serve
1 tablespoon olive oil, plus extra for drizzling
70 g (2½ oz) trimmed kale, sliced
250 g (9 oz) new potatoes
150 g (5½ oz) raw chorizo, skin removed and thinly sliced
1 large onion, halved and sliced
a generous pinch of smoked paprika
1 rosemary sprig, leaves chopped
1 marjoram sprig, leaves chopped
fine sea salt
freshly ground black pepper

First, get the octopus on the go. Slice off the heads and add to a saucepan along with the tentacles. Add the vegetable stock and lemon slices, and top up with enough cold water to cover well. Gently simmer for 25–30 minutes or until the octopus is tender. Drain, then cut any large tentacles in half – you want bite-sized pieces. Drizzle with olive oil and set aside.

While the octopus is cooking, blanch the kale in boiling salted water for 1 minute, then set aside in a colander to drain and dry.

Boil the potatoes in salted water until just tender, then drain. When cool enough to handle, slice them into 1 cm (½ inch) rounds and spread on a plate to dry out a little.

Now, heat the 1 tablespoon of olive oil in a frying pan. Add the chorizo and fry until cooked through and starting to crisp around the edges. Scoop out of the frying pan with a slotted spoon and set aside. Add the onion, paprika, rosemary and marjoram to the same pan – you should have lots of chorizo-infused oil left – and fry over medium–low heat for about 8 minutes or until the onion is very soft and tender.

Increase the heat, add the kale, octopus, chorizo and potatoes to the pan, and season with sea salt and black pepper. Gently stir to combine – you need to use more of a folding action, really, so as not to break up the potatoes. Fry until everything starts to take on some colour and is coated in a slick of the chorizo-infused oil (you might need to add a splash more olive oil).

Serve immediately, with a little lemon juice squeezed over the top and more salt and pepper to taste.

Skordalia comes in all different guises in Greece, made either with potatoes or bread, but always loaded with garlic and olive oil. It's a rich sauce rather than a side order of mashed potato, so you don't need loads. If you don't have a potato ricer, use a masher or push the potatoes through a sieve. Don't put them in a food processor or you'll end up with glue.

Sea bass with saffron skordalia

Serves 4

4 sea bass or barramundi fillets
sea salt
freshly ground black pepper
2 tablespoons olive oil

For the skordalia
300 g (10½ oz) boiling potatoes, peeled and cubed
a pinch of saffron threads
2 garlic cloves
20 g (¾ oz) toasted almonds
1 tablespoon lemon juice, or to taste
185 ml (6 fl oz/¾ cup) olive oil
sea salt
freshly ground black pepper

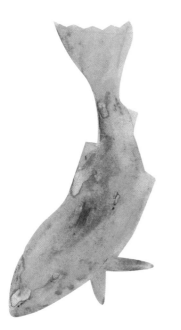

First, make the skordalia. Boil the potatoes in salted water until very tender. Drain, keeping 250 ml (9 fl oz/1 cup) of the cooking water. Crush the potatoes back into the saucepan with a potato ricer, or use a masher, and stir with a wooden spoon until creamy. Cover to keep warm and set aside.

Put the saffron in a mortar with a splash of the potato water and pound until the saffron is dissolved. Transfer to a food processor, then add the garlic, almonds, lemon juice and olive oil. Blitz until you have a creamy, egg-yolk coloured mixture. Pour the mixture into the potatoes and stir to combine, adding some more of the potato water to achieve a smooth sauce. Have a taste and season with sea salt and black pepper, and add more lemon juice if you like. Cover and set aside to keep warm.

Now, cook your fish. Score each fillet three or four times across the skin, pat dry with paper towel and generously season with sea salt and black pepper on both sides. Heat a frying pan over medium–high heat, add enough olive oil to coat the pan and then add the fish, skin side down. Press down with a spatula or fish slice so that the fish lies completely flat in the pan. Cook for 2–4 minutes or until almost cooked through (the exact time will depend on the thickness of your fish). Flip the fish, remove the pan from the heat and allow the fish to finish cooking in the pan's residual heat for 1 minute.

Serve the fish immediately, with a generous spoonful of skordalia on the side, and a bowl of Shaved zucchini with lemon herb dressing and walnuts (page 79) or Wheat grain tabouleh with chervil and mint (page 72).

Red mullet are probably my favourite fish – gorgeous to look at, with shimmering pinky–gold skin and sweet, delicate flesh. These beauties don't need elaborate cooking, so this is a simple recipe that relies on excellent ingredients – especially the fish, tomatoes and olive oil. I suppose you could substitute frozen broad beans for fresh, but in all honesty they taste mealy and bland by comparison, so I wouldn't.

Roast whole red mullet with tomato, fennel and olive salad

Serves 4

4 large or 8 small red mullet, cleaned, scaled and gutted
juice of 1 orange
juice of 1 lemon
2 tablespoons chopped lemon thyme or thyme leaves
3 garlic cloves, crushed
sea salt flakes
freshly ground black pepper

For the salad

300 g (10½ oz) ripe mixed cherry or small tomatoes, halved
1½ teaspoons sea salt flakes
45 g (1½ oz) fennel bulb with fronds
lemon juice, for sprinkling
250 g (9 oz) podded broad beans
90 g (3¼ oz) wrinkled black or kalamata olives
10 mint leaves, thinly sliced

For the salad dressing

2 teaspoons finely chopped oregano leaves
2 tablespoons extra virgin olive oil, or to taste
1 tablespoon lemon juice, or to taste
a whisper of grated garlic

First, start on the salad. Put the tomatoes in a colander set over a bowl, sprinkle with the sea salt and toss. Set aside to drain for 30 minutes. Thinly slice the fennel bulb, reserving a few of the fronds, and sprinkle with lemon juice to prevent browning.

Put the salad dressing ingredients in a screw-top jar and shake until well combined. Put to one side for the flavours to mingle.

Next, prepare the fish. Preheat the oven to 220°C (425°F). Cut two to three diagonal slashes in both sides of each fish, being careful not to cut too deeply into the flesh. Put the fish in a ceramic or glass ovenproof dish that is just large enough to hold them snugly. Whisk together the orange juice, lemon juice, thyme, garlic, sea salt and black pepper to make the marinade. Pour over the fish and rub the thyme into the slashes, turning the fish over to coat well. Roast for 12–15 minutes or until the fish is cooked through.

While the fish is cooking, simmer the broad beans in a pan of boiling salted water for 2 minutes or until just tender. Drain and plunge into cold water, then slip the beans from their grey skins to reveal the gleaming emerald beans. Put the beans in a bowl and add the tomatoes, sliced fennel, olives and mint. Toss with enough of the dressing to generously coat – have a taste and add more salt, pepper, lemon juice or olive oil if you think the seasoning needs adjusting.

Serve the fish sprinkled with the reserved fennel fronds, with the beautiful salad alongside.

Pasta, beans, rice & grains

We used to spend our holidays at a self-catering farmhouse in Italy and I once asked the wonderful owner, an amazing cook named Paolo, if we could have some basil. He proudly took us through the kitchen to his herb garden and indicated with a sweep of his arm at least a dozen different types of basil. 'What kind would you like?' he asked, as if it were the most obvious question in the world. I'd never seen anything like it and I will never forget the intoxicating perfume of those herbs. Basil still reminds me of summer and remains my favourite herb by a long stretch.

Penne with zucchini, burrata and basil dressing

Serves 4

500 g (1 lb 2 oz) baby zucchini (courgettes), cut into rounds
½ teaspoon fine sea salt
3 tablespoons olive oil
2 garlic cloves, bruised with the side of a knife
350 g (12 oz) penne
200 g (7 oz) ball of burrata cheese

For the dressing

50 g (1¾ oz) basil leaves
10 g (¼ oz) mint leaves
30 ml (1 fl oz) white balsamic vinegar, or to taste
3 tablespoons extra virgin olive oil
sea salt flakes
freshly ground black pepper

Put the zucchini in a colander set over a bowl, sprinkle over the salt and set aside for 20 minutes.

Pat the zucchini dry with paper towel. Warm the olive oil in a frying pan and toss in the garlic cloves. Stir around in the pan for a minute or so until the cloves start to sizzle and take on a little colour, then scoop out with a slotted spoon and discard. Add the zucchini to the garlicky oil and slowly cook over medium heat, turning now and then, for about 20 minutes or until golden and meltingly soft.

While the zucchini is cooking, start boiling some salted water for the pasta and then make the dressing. Put the basil, mint, balsamic vinegar and olive oil in a food processor, season with sea salt and black pepper, and blitz until smooth – some flecks of herbs are lovely. Have a taste and then add more salt, pepper or vinegar if needed – the dressing should be very mildly sharp. Put the dressing to one side and then cook the pasta according to the packet instructions.

To assemble, drain the pasta, keeping a little of the cooking liquid. Tip the pasta into the frying pan with the zucchini. Pour in half the dressing and quickly and gently toss so that everything is coated in a slick of vibrant green. Add a splash of the cooking liquid if the pasta is looking at all dry.

Divide the pasta among four serving bowls and very quickly tear up the burrata and place on top – ideally you need to do this while the pasta is still hot so the cheese melts a little. Drizzle the remaining dressing over the top and serve immediately.

The bitterness of the witlof and the saltiness of the bacon – tamed a bit by loads of lemon – is a combination that makes my mouth dance. I absolutely love the bright freshness of this pasta: it's a wonderfully light meal. Use radicchio if you can't find red witlof – they're from the same family. If you're very organised and have everything prepped first (I'm rarely that clever, by the way) the pasta will be cooked at the same time as the rest of the dish.

Spaghetti with red witlof, bacon and garlic crumbs

Serves 4

400 g (14 oz) spaghetti
1 tablespoon olive oil, plus extra for cooking
2 thick rashers smoked bacon, cut into matchsticks
250 g (9 oz) red witlof (chicory), thinly sliced with a few of the end parts of the red leaves torn
2 tablespoons dry white wine
finely grated zest of 1 lemon
1 small handful flat-leaf parsley leaves

For the garlic crumbs
1 tablespoon olive oil
30 g (1 oz/½ cup) good-quality fresh breadcrumbs, ideally made from sourdough or Olive oil bread (page 19)
a pinch of sea salt flakes
2 garlic cloves, crushed
finely grated zest of 1 lemon

Get the water for your pasta on the go – don't add too much salt as salty bacon is in play here. While it's coming to the boil, make the garlic crumbs. Heat the olive oil in a large frying pan, add the breadcrumbs and a pinch of sea salt, and stir-fry over high heat until the breadcrumbs just start to smell toasty, about 3 minutes. Add the garlic and cook, stirring to stop it burning, for a couple of minutes more. Pull the frying pan off the heat and stir in the grated lemon zest, then spread the breadcrumbs out on a plate so they stay crisp. Wipe out the pan.

Add the pasta to the boiling water, then heat the olive oil in the frying pan. Add the bacon and fry over medium heat until starting to turn golden. Add the sliced witlof and fry for a few minutes more, stirring often, until it is just softened. Pour in the wine. While it's bubbling up, scrape the bottom of the pan with a wooden spoon to loosen any delicious caramelised bits. Pull the pan off the heat.

When the pasta is cooked, drain it, keeping a little of the cooking liquid. Tip the pasta into the frying pan, return to low heat and add a splash of the olive oil and a splash of the cooking liquid. Gently toss to combine and warm the pasta through, adding more oil or liquid if the pasta is dry.

Add the lemon zest, parsley, torn witlof and half the garlic crumbs to the frying pan, then gently toss. Serve immediately, with the remaining garlic crumbs sprinkled over the top.

Traditionally, freshly cracked walnuts are used to make this sensational pasta sauce, and purists would say it's the only way to go. If you use fresh ready-shelled walnuts I think the results are still fantastic and it means this dish can be on the table within 20 minutes.

Farfalle with creamy walnut pesto

Serves 4

400 g (14 oz) farfalle
140 ml (4½ fl oz) extra virgin
    olive oil, plus extra for
    drizzling
150 g (5½ oz/1¼ cups) walnuts
40 g (1½ oz) good-quality
    country-style bread
30 g (1 oz) parmesan cheese,
    grated
1 large garlic clove
180 g (6 oz) Greek-style
    yoghurt
2 tablespoons milk
1½ teaspoons sherry vinegar
a generous squeeze of
    lemon juice
sea salt flakes

Cook the pasta in boiling salted water according to the packet instructions. Drain well, keeping a little of the cooking liquid, then drizzle with olive oil and toss to coat.

While this is happening, blitz the remaining ingredients in a food processor until creamy, adding water to loosen the sauce to a soft dropping consistency, if necessary. Have a taste and add more salt or lemon juice.

Toss the pasta with most of the walnut sauce and a splash of the pasta water to loosen. Serve immediately, with the remaining sauce spooned over the top.

Simple, simple, simple. Everyone needs a recipe like this in their cooking arsenal: something you don't need to labour over and that goes from pan to plate in 10 minutes, or however long it takes to cook the pasta. Broccolini, similar to broccoli but more dainty and with long thin stalks, is perfect here as it cooks in a flash. Even the thicker stalks are delicious, so there's no waste. A perfect, healthy weeknight dinner.

Penne with broccolini, goat's curd and smashed pistachios

Serves 4

400 g (14 oz) penne
2 tablespoons olive oil, plus extra for drizzling
200 g (7 oz) broccolini, cut into florets, larger stems sliced
sea salt flakes
freshly ground black pepper
a pinch of chilli flakes
finely grated zest of 1 lemon, plus a squeeze of lemon juice
60 g (2¼ oz) pistachio nuts, toasted and roughly chopped
200 g (7 oz) goat's curd or soft goat's cheese

First, cook the pasta in boiling salted water according to the packet instructions. Drain, keeping a little of the cooking liquid, then drizzle with olive oil and toss to coat.

Now, blanch the broccolini in boiling salted water for 30 seconds. Drain, rinse in cold water to halt the cooking, then drain again. Heat the 2 tablespoons olive oil in a frying pan. Add the broccolini, season with sea salt and black pepper, and stir-fry over medium–high heat until just cooked through and slightly coloured – just a minute or two. Reduce the heat to low and stir in the chilli flakes, lemon zest and lemon juice.

Add the pasta, toss to combine with the broccolini, then add most of the pistachios, three-quarters of the goat's curd or goat's cheese in spoonfuls or pieces, and a splash of the pasta cooking water. Gently fold everything together until well combined and the goat's curd or cheese has melted into a light sauce, adding more of the pasta cooking water if needed. Taste for seasoning and add more salt and pepper if necessary.

Serve the pasta immediately, dotted with the remaining goat's curd or cheese and sprinkled with the remaining pistachios.

Stewing eggplant brings out its rich, almost meaty flavour and this is one of my favourite ways to eat it. In fact, it's a great dish if you're trying to cut down on meat, or for when you're feeding vegetarians and carnivores at the same sitting.

Rigatoni with rich eggplant sauce

Serves 4

1 eggplant (aubergine),
   about 400 g (14 oz)
1 teaspoon fine sea salt
olive oil, for shallow-frying,
   plus extra for drizzling
1 onion, finely chopped
sea salt flakes
2 garlic cloves, crushed
1 teaspoon dried oregano
¼ teaspoon chilli flakes
500 ml (17 fl oz/2 cups)
   tomato passata
3 tablespoons red wine
freshly ground black pepper
400 g (14 oz) rigatoni
1 handful basil leaves
grated parmesan cheese,
   to serve (optional)

Start by preparing the eggplant – cut it into 1.5 cm (⅝ inch) cubes, place in a colander set over a bowl and toss with the fine sea salt. Leave to drain for 20 minutes so that some of the water is drawn out, then pat dry with paper towel. Heat enough olive oil in a frying pan to come 2 cm (¾ inch) up the side and fry the eggplant until golden all over. Scoop out with a slotted spoon and transfer to a plate lined with paper towel.

Pour the oil out of the pan into a small bowl, wipe out with paper towel, then pour 2 tablespoons of the oil back in. Set the pan over medium heat. When the oil is hot, add the onion and a pinch of sea salt. Very gently fry the onion for 10 minutes or until very soft. Add the garlic, oregano and chilli flakes, and fry for another couple of minutes, making sure the garlic doesn't burn. Stir in the passata and wine, and season with sea salt and black pepper. Bring to the boil, then reduce the heat and gently simmer for 20 minutes, stirring now and then.

About 10 minutes before the sauce has finished cooking, cook the pasta in boiling salted water according to the packet instructions. Lightly drain, reserving some of the cooking liquid, then return the pasta to the pan with a drizzle of olive oil to prevent sticking.

When the sauce is cooked, add the fried eggplant cubes and warm through for a couple of minutes. Pull the pan off the heat, tear the basil leaves and fold through the sauce. Add the pasta to the pan and toss, adding some of the reserved cooking liquid to loosen if needed. Serve immediately, with grated parmesan (if using).

I make this so often, I can't tell you: it tastes delicious, looks gorgeous and can be served in loads of different ways. If I'm feeding vegetarians it's perfect, as it makes a wholesome main meal for them, and I might cook some meat or chicken to go with it for the carnivores. Use farro or other grains if you can't get hold of freekeh, but for me its distinctive nutty flavour really makes this special, so it's worth trying to lay your hands on some.

Freekeh with feta, roast tomatoes and herbs

Serves 4–6 as a side

200 g (7 oz) cracked freekeh
1 teaspoon fine sea salt, plus extra for seasoning
3 tablespoons olive oil
175 g (6 oz) mixed cherry tomatoes
¼ teaspoon ground cumin
¼ teaspoon smoked paprika
freshly ground black pepper
1 large onion, halved and thinly sliced
1 red capsicum (pepper), chopped
1 tablespoon tomato paste (concentrated purée)
a generous pinch of cayenne pepper
150 g (5½ oz) greens such as silverbeet (Swiss chard), spring greens, beetroot greens, savoy cabbage or kale, thinly sliced
finely grated zest of ½ lemon
2 handfuls mint leaves, chopped
1 handful parsley or coriander (cilantro) leaves, chopped
200 g (7 oz) feta cheese, cut into cubes
extra virgin olive oil, for drizzling

Preheat the oven to 200°C (400°F).

Put the freekeh in a saucepan and cover with 1 litre (35 fl oz/4 cups) water. Add the salt and 3 teaspoons of the olive oil and bring to the boil, then reduce the heat to low, cover and cook for 25–30 minutes or until the grains are tender. Most of the water should be absorbed by this time, but drain off any excess. Set aside in a sieve set over a bowl so the grains dry out a little and drain completely.

While the freekeh is cooking, put the tomatoes in an ovenproof dish, sprinkle with the cumin and paprika, generously season with sea salt and black pepper, and drizzle with another 3 teaspoons of the olive oil. Toss to coat the tomatoes in the spices and oil, then roast for about 10 minutes or until the skins have burst and the tomatoes are just tender. Set aside.

Meanwhile, warm the remaining 30 ml (1 fl oz) olive oil in a frying pan over medium–low heat and add the onion and capsicum. Gently cook for about 15 minutes or until the onion is golden brown and soft. Stir in the tomato paste and cayenne pepper, and cook for a couple of minutes until you can smell the tomato paste starting to caramelise. Add the greens and a splash of water and toss so all the ingredients are well combined. Reduce the heat to low, cover (use a baking tray if your pan doesn't have a lid) and cook until the greens are just tender.

To assemble, combine the freekeh with the onion and greens mixture, the lemon zest and most of the herbs. Tip out onto a serving platter and check for seasoning, adding more salt and pepper if necessary. Gently fold in the feta, then arrange the tomatoes on top and spoon on any tomato juices left in the roasting tin. Drizzle with extra virgin olive oil and sprinkle over the remaining herbs to serve.

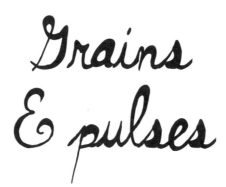

Grains & pulses

Hardly a family meal goes by in the Mediterranean without grains and pulses being served, and in countless delicious guises. Made into bread, pasta and risotto; tossed into salads and stirred into stews; or served plain and simple as a side dish to soak up sauces ... whichever way they are served, grains and pulses are fundamental to the traditional Mediterranean diet.

But that's not to say that filling your meals with pasta and bread is the healthy course. On a traditional Mediterranean table, pasta is commonly a side dish served alongside meat or poultry and lots of vegetables. Bread is essential, of course, but also in moderation. One of the best ways to eat Mediterranean-style is to add more whole grains and pulses to your everyday cooking – not to binge on spaghetti.

This is easier to do than ever. In recent years, grains such as freekeh, farro, spelt, barley and wheat grain that were once unfamiliar have become readily available alongside rice, burghul (bulgur) and couscous. Baked beans were once the closest many of us came to pulses, but now a gorgeous array of lentils, chickpeas and beans (cannellini, broad, black and butterbeans, to name just a few) fill the supermarket shelves. This is good news, as eating a wide range of grains and pulses is the best way to consume a broad spectrum of vitamins and minerals.

Admittedly, some grains and pulses take a long time to cook and most pulses need soaking first. That's why I like to cook a big batch and keep them in the freezer until I need them. Grains soak up flavours beautifully, so toss them with dressings, pan juices or sauces and add vegetables, nuts, seeds and a little meat or fish. Protein- and fibre-rich beans are fantastic to bulk up stews and soups, especially if you're trying to reduce your meat intake.

Gigantes plakie – giant baked beans – is the dish my children love most when we visit Greece, and it's up there on my list of favourites. We love the beans as much for their comical size as their deliciousness: they're meaty, creamy and a sponge for the flavours they're cooked in. Dried gigantes beans can be hard to find, but it's worth buying them online or from speciality shops. Or use large butterbeans instead. I often soak and cook a large batch of dried beans, then freeze what I'm not using immediately. I then have a stash ready to use, and here I'll pop them straight into the onion mixture with the passata.

Gigantes beans and haloumi in spicy tomato sauce

Serves 4–6

200 g (7 oz) dried gigantes beans, soaked overnight
1 carrot, cut into 3 pieces
1 celery stalk, cut into 3 pieces
2 bay leaves
2 tablespoons olive oil, plus extra for drizzling
1 large onion, finely chopped
½ red capsicum (pepper), chopped
sea salt flakes
1–3 teaspoons harissa paste, or to taste
2 tablespoons tomato paste (concentrated purée)
1 heaped teaspoon dried oregano
300 ml (10½ fl oz) tomato passata
freshly ground black pepper
250 g (9 oz) haloumi cheese, cut into 1 cm (½ inch) slices

Rinse and drain the beans, put them in a large saucepan and cover with lots of cold water, then add the carrot, celery and bay leaves. Bring to the boil, then reduce the heat and simmer for 45 minutes to 1 hour or until slightly tender but not soft – the exact time will depend on the age of the beans. Drain, keeping 200 ml (7 fl oz) of the cooking liquid, and discard the bay leaves, carrot and celery (or use the vegetables in another dish).

Preheat the oven to 160°C (315°F).

While the beans are cooking, warm the olive oil in a frying pan over medium heat. Add the onion, capsicum and a pinch of sea salt, and fry for 8 minutes. Add the harissa paste and tomato paste, and stir around in the onion mixture for a couple of minutes, then add the oregano, beans, passata, cooking liquid, and sea salt and black pepper. Tip the mixture into an ovenproof dish, cover with a double layer of foil and bake for 1 hour.

Remove the dish from the oven and check on the sauce – if it looks a little dry, stir in a splash of water. Tuck the haloumi slices into the bean mixture, cover with the foil and cook for a further 45 minutes. Drizzle with a little more olive oil to serve.

Rich, flavourful, filling and warming, this is the perfect dish for a cold day. It's reminiscent of risotto but made with the grain-shaped pasta called orzo in Italy and *kritharáki* in Greece instead of rice. It's also baked in the oven rather than stirred on the stove. I've tried this dish with cuttlefish or largish squid and the results aren't so good, as the rice cooks before the seafood. Baby squid are perfect and come out beautifully tender. This is quite a rich dish so the portions are not enormous. It's perfect with a bowl of simple greens or crisp salad leaves.

Baked orzo with squid

Serves 4

2 tablespoons olive oil
1 onion, finely chopped
sea salt flakes
1 tablespoon tomato paste
  (concentrated purée)
2 garlic cloves, thinly sliced
1½ teaspoons caraway seeds
½ teaspoon ground allspice
400 g (14 oz) baby squid, cut
  into 1 cm (½ inch) rings,
  tentacles left whole
200 ml (7 fl oz) red wine
250 ml (9 fl oz/1 cup) tomato
  passata
200 g (7 oz) orzo
2 bay leaves
a pinch of sugar
freshly ground black pepper

Preheat the oven to 180°C (350°F).

Heat the olive oil in a flameproof casserole dish over medium heat and fry the onion with a generous pinch of sea salt until soft, about 8 minutes. Stir in the tomato paste, sliced garlic, caraway seeds and allspice, and cook for 3 minutes or until aromatic. Add the squid and stir to combine.

Pour in the red wine and let it bubble away for a minute or so, then add the passata and 500 ml (17 fl oz/2 cups) water. Add the orzo, bay leaves, sugar and some sea salt and black pepper, and stir well. The orzo should be completely covered in liquid. Bring to a very gentle boil, then cover and transfer to the oven for 25–30 minutes or until the orzo and squid are tender. Check halfway through cooking and add a little more water if the sauce looks like it's drying out.

Remove from the oven and let the orzo and squid sit for 5 minutes before dividing them among serving bowls.

This is a delicious and filling meal on its own but also makes a wonderful side dish for fish, chicken or lamb. My children love it – for them, I think it has echoes of fried rice, so it's an excellent way to get some good grains into their diet. You can mix up the grains if you want, and use barley, farro or wild rice if you prefer – adjust the cooking times accordingly. You'll have a couple of pots going at the same time, but this recipe is really pretty easy.

Lentils, rice and chickpeas with caramelised fennel and garlic yoghurt

Serves 2–4 as a side

100 g (3½ oz) puy lentils or
   tiny blue-green lentils
2 bay leaves
750 ml (26 fl oz/3 cups)
   chicken or vegetable stock
2 garlic cloves
70 g (2½ oz) brown rice
a pinch of saffron threads
3 tablespoons olive oil, plus
   extra for drizzling
1 large fennel bulb, about 250 g
   (9 oz), thinly sliced
1 teaspoon ras el hanout
1 teaspoon ground turmeric
½ teaspoon ground cumin
a pinch of cayenne pepper
sea salt
110 g (3¾ oz) cooked or tinned
   chickpeas, rinsed and drained
180 g (6 oz) Greek-style
   yoghurt
1 handful mint leaves, chopped,
   plus extra for sprinkling
finely grated zest of ½ lemon
freshly ground black pepper

Combine the lentils, bay leaves and stock in a saucepan. Bruise one of the garlic cloves with the side of a knife and add it to the pan. Bring to the boil, then reduce the heat to a simmer and cook for 20–30 minutes or until the lentils are tender but not mushy. Drain, keeping the cooking liquid, then discard the bay leaves and garlic.

While the lentils are cooking, put the rice and saffron in a saucepan and cover with 185 ml (6 fl oz/¾ cup) water. Bring to the boil, then reduce the heat to low, cover and simmer for about 20 minutes or until tender. Drain off any remaining water.

While the grains are cooking, warm 2 tablespoons of the olive oil in a frying pan over medium heat. Add the fennel, spices and a generous pinch of sea salt. Stir over medium heat for a couple of minutes until the fennel is coated in the oil and is starting to soften. Add a splash of water, reduce the heat to low and cover with a lid or baking tray. Cook for 20 minutes, stirring now and then (add more water if it is becoming dry) until the fennel is very tender. Uncover, increase the heat and fry until the fennel starts to caramelise and become crisp.

Remove half the fennel and set aside, then add the chickpeas, rice, lentils and remaining oil to the pan. Toss, adding a generous splash of the lentil cooking liquid to moisten. Stir over medium heat for 1 minute, then pull off the heat, cover and set aside for 10 minutes.

While this is happening, crush the remaining garlic clove and stir into the yoghurt with a pinch of sea salt.

Add the mint and lemon zest to the grains and chickpeas, and taste for seasoning, adding sea salt and black pepper if needed. Tip onto a serving platter, then top with the yoghurt and remaining fennel, and sprinkle with mint. Serve warm or at room temperature.

Farro is such a beautiful wheat grain, bursting with fibre, protein and other good things, as well as being chewy and delicious. If you can't find it, substitute it with spelt, although it's much softer. This is a glorious autumnal or winter dish, and one that I often adapt according to what I have by way of vegetables. Keep the beetroot in, as its colour is lovely against the grains and adds earthy sweetness. I haven't included them in the recipe below, but the Confit shallots with herbs and garlic (page 153) are absolutely wonderful tossed into the mix as well.

Warm salad of farro, roasted vegetables and chestnuts

Serves 4–6 as a side

150 g (5½ oz) celeriac
150 g (5½ oz) carrots
200 g (7 oz) raw beetroot
3 tablespoons olive oil
2 tablespoons honey
1 teaspoon sumac
leaves from 1 lemon thyme
   or thyme sprig
½ teaspoon sea salt flakes,
   plus extra for seasoning
freshly ground black pepper
50 g (1¾ oz) vacuum-packed
   chestnuts
140 g (5 oz) pearled farro
2 tablespoons mixed seeds,
   such as pepitas (pumpkin
   seeds) and sunflower seeds
1 handful flat-leaf parsley
   leaves, roughly chopped
extra virgin olive oil, for
   drizzling

For the dressing

2 tablespoons white balsamic
   vinegar
2 tablespoons extra virgin
   olive oil
2 tablespoons walnut oil
1 tablespoon honey

First, get your vegetables on the go. Preheat the oven to 200°C (400°F). Peel the celeriac, carrots and beetroot, and cut them into 3 cm (1¼ inch) chunks. Pop the vegetables into a large roasting tin in a single layer. Whisk together 2 tablespoons of the olive oil, the honey, sumac and thyme, season with sea salt and black pepper, and pour over the vegetables. Toss to coat. Roast for 30 minutes, then add the chestnuts, shaking to coat them in the oil. Roast for 15 minutes more or until everything is softened and golden.

While the vegetables are roasting, put the farro, the ½ teaspoon sea salt and the remaining 1 tablespoon oil in a saucepan. Pour in 700 ml (24 fl oz) water and simmer for 20–25 minutes or until the grains are tender – bear in mind that farro retains some bite and chewiness when cooked. If the water is absorbed before the grains are done, add a little boiling water; if there is excess liquid when cooked, drain this off.

While the grains are cooking, make the dressing – just put all the ingredients in a screw-top jar and shake well.

As soon as the farro is ready, add half the dressing and toss – do this while the grains are still hot so they absorb the flavours. Set aside to keep warm.

Transfer the cooked vegetables to a serving platter or bowl. Add the farro, seeds and most of the parsley. Gently toss with enough of the remaining dressing to generously coat. Taste for seasoning and add more salt and pepper if necessary – the farro might need quite a bit of salt. Serve warm or at room temperature, scattered with the remaining parsley and drizzled with extra virgin olive oil.

This is more like a risotto than a pilaf because it's quite creamy, but it uses long-grain rice instead of risotto rice, so you still get some bite from the grains. It's very simple, very soothing and works well as a side to meat or chicken, but I also find it a comforting bowlful to enjoy on its own. Goat's butter is widely available these days and adds a lovely richness, so it's well worth tracking down.

Wild rice pilaf with leeks and goat's butter

Serves 4

1 tablespoon olive oil
40 g (1½ oz) goat's butter
4 leeks, white and pale green parts only, sliced into thin discs
3 spring onions (scallions), thinly sliced
2 garlic cloves, thinly sliced
100 g (3½ oz/½ cup) wild rice
200 g (7 oz/1 cup) brown rice
3 tablespoons lemon juice
800 ml (28 fl oz) vegetable stock
30 g (1 oz) pine nuts, toasted
1 handful flat-leaf parsley leaves, finely chopped
1 handful dill, finely chopped
sea salt
freshly ground black pepper

Heat the olive oil and half of the goat's butter in a saucepan over medium heat. Fry the sliced leeks, spring onions and garlic until soft, about 5 minutes. Add the wild rice and brown rice, and stir for 2 minutes or until the grains are coated in the oil.

Pour in the lemon juice and stock. Bring to the boil, then reduce the heat to low and cook until the grains are tender, stirring now and then to stop the grains sticking to the bottom of the pan. Pull off the heat and drain off any excess liquid.

Stir in the pine nuts, herbs and remaining goat's butter. Cover and set to one side for 10 minutes, then season with sea salt and black pepper, and serve immediately.

Black lentils, or beluga lentils as they're sometimes known, are a speciality of Sicily but are now grown elsewhere and widely available. The little jewels are richly flavoured and seem to absorb flavours better than other lentils, and they look pleasingly dramatic in the bowl. The flavours in this dish are delicious – the tarragon transforms it into something special. It makes a perfectly lovely main meal on its own, but we often serve it as a side to chicken or fish.

Black lentils with sweet potato and tarragon-walnut dressing

Serves 2–4 as a side

400 g (14 oz) sweet potato, cut into 1.5 cm (⅝ inch) cubes
2 tablespoons olive oil
sea salt flakes
freshly ground black pepper
1 large onion, finely chopped
2 garlic cloves, finely chopped
200 g (7 oz) black lentils
750 ml (26 fl oz/3 cups) chicken or vegetable stock

For the dressing

3 tablespoons extra virgin olive oil
2 tablespoons walnut oil
2 tablespoons white balsamic vinegar
1 teaspoon honey
60 g (2¼ oz/½ cup) toasted walnuts, chopped
1 tablespoon finely chopped tarragon leaves
1 garlic clove, crushed
sea salt flakes
freshly ground black pepper

Preheat the oven to 180°C (350°F). Pop the sweet potato into a large roasting tin, toss with 3 teaspoons of the olive oil and generously season with sea salt and black pepper. Spread the sweet potato out in a single layer – the more space the pieces have around them the more they will crisp up – and roast for 45 minutes or until tender and starting to brown at the edges.

While this is happening, heat the remaining olive oil in a saucepan and fry the onion and garlic over medium heat for a few minutes or until starting to soften. Stir in the lentils and stock, then simmer for about 20 minutes or until tender – it might take less or more time depending on the lentils. Keep some freshly boiled water to hand and add a splash to the pan if the liquid evaporates before the lentils are tender. The idea is to end up with almost no liquid left by the time the lentils are cooked – just enough to keep them wet without turning soggy.

While the lentils are bubbling away, make the dressing. Simply put all the ingredients in a largish screw-top jar and shake well. Have a taste and add more salt and pepper if needed. Stir the dressing into the lentils as soon as they are cooked – they will absorb the flavours better when hot – and set aside to keep warm.

When the sweet potato is cooked, fold through the lentils. Serve warm or at room temperature.

Risotto made with starchy medium- or short-grain rice is lovely, but I prefer spelt, an ancient wheat grain, for its mild nutty flavour and slightly chewy texture. It's just more interesting. I've added nettles here because they're a lovely springtime addition and are packed with vitamins and other nutrients. They're widely available at markets these days, or pick them yourself: collect just the top five or six leaves on each spear (wear sturdy gloves!), then wash and rinse well. Once the nettles hit the heat, the stings disappear.

Spelt risotto with pea and nettle purée

Serves 4

3 tablespoons olive oil
200 g (7 oz/1⅓ cups) fresh
    or frozen peas
1 handful washed nettle tops
    or baby English spinach
    leaves, tough stalks removed
sea salt flakes
1 litre (35 fl oz/4 cups) hot
    vegetable stock, plus extra
    if needed
1 small handful mint leaves,
    chopped
freshly ground black pepper
4 French shallots, finely
    chopped
1 fat garlic clove, finely chopped
300 g (10½ oz) pearled spelt
200 ml (7 fl oz) white wine
30 g (1 oz) parmesan or
    pecorino cheese, grated
finely grated zest of ½ lemon
freshly ground black pepper
3 tablespoons goat's curd
pea shoots, to serve
extra virgin olive oil, for
    drizzling

First, prepare the pea and nettle purée. Heat half the olive oil in a frying pan and add 130 g (4½ oz) of the peas, all of the nettles or spinach and a generous pinch of sea salt. Fry for 5 minutes (or less if using frozen peas) or until almost tender. Add 150 ml (5 fl oz) of the stock and the mint, and simmer until the liquid has reduced by half and the peas are very soft. Tip the mixture into a blender, season with sea salt and black pepper, and blitz to a smooth purée, adding a little more stock if needed to loosen. Set aside.

Now, heat the remaining olive oil in a saucepan and fry the shallots over medium heat with a pinch of sea salt until soft but not coloured, about 5 minutes. Add the garlic and fry for a few minutes more. Tip in the spelt and stir for a couple of minutes to coat in the oil. Pour in the wine and stir until absorbed. Reduce the heat to a simmer and start pouring in the remaining stock a little at a time while stirring, adding just enough to cover the grains and waiting for the liquid to be absorbed before adding more. When you've added three-quarters of the stock, tip in the remaining peas, then continue adding the stock as before until the spelt and peas are tender. The mixture should be quite wet, not thick and sticky, so add enough stock to loosen it once the grains are cooked if necessary.

Pull the pan off the heat and stir in the pea and nettle purée, the parmesan or pecorino cheese and the lemon zest. Have a taste and add sea salt and black pepper if needed.

To serve, spoon the risotto into four bowls, dot with the goat's curd and top with the pea shoots. Drizzle with extra virgin olive oil and serve immediately.

Vegetables

Artichoke and broad bean stew is a Greek classic but my version is lighter and sings with fresh flavours. Use drained artichokes from a jar if you're short of time, in which case you can ignore the method for cooking them. The sprightly flavour and texture of fresh baby artichokes is preferable. Don't use big globe artichokes as they are fiddlier to prepare and you need to remove the chokes.

Artichokes with broad beans, preserved lemon and almonds

Serves 4 as a generous side

1 lemon
20 baby artichokes
600 ml (21 fl oz) dry white wine
250 ml (9 fl oz/1 cup) olive oil
4 bay leaves
4 garlic cloves, bruised
400 g (14 oz) podded broad
  beans
2 large handfuls mint leaves,
  chopped
8 dill sprigs, chopped
80 g (2¾ oz/½ cup) blanched
  almonds, lightly toasted
3 tablespoons chopped
  preserved lemon rind
sea salt flakes
freshly ground black pepper
Manchego or parmesan cheese
  shavings, to serve (optional)
good-quality extra virgin olive
  oil, for drizzling

For the dressing

3 tablespoons white balsamic
  vinegar
90 ml (3 fl oz) grapeseed or
  other flavourless oil
90 ml (3 fl oz) extra virgin
  olive oil
sea salt flakes
freshly ground black pepper

Start by preparing the artichokes. Use a vegetable peeler to peel off the lemon zest in strips and set aside. Half-fill a large bowl with cold water, then squeeze in the lemon juice. Trim the artichoke stalks to about 2 cm (¾ inch) long, then remove the tough outer leaves to reveal the tender inner heart. Use a vegetable peeler to remove the outside of the stalk, then cut off the top third of each artichoke – I know it seems like a waste but the central heart is the only tasty part. Add the trimmed artichokes to the lemony water as you go to prevent them discolouring.

Pour the wine, olive oil and 600 ml (21 fl oz) water into a large saucepan and add the lemon zest, bay leaves and garlic. Drain the artichokes and add these to the pan. Bring to the boil, then reduce the heat to low and cook with the lid on for 15 minutes or until fork tender. Remove the artichokes with a slotted spoon and set aside to cool. Fish out the garlic cloves, finely chop and set to one side.

While the artichokes are cooling, cook the broad beans in boiling salted water until tender, about 2 minutes, then drain and refresh in cool water. Slip the beans from their papery skins – not strictly necessary with tender young broad beans but worth it to expose their gorgeous emerald colour. Set aside to cool.

For the dressing, pop the ingredients plus the reserved chopped garlic cloves into a screw-top jar and shake until well combined.

On a large shallow plate or serving bowl, gently toss together the artichokes, broad beans, herbs, half the almonds, preserved lemon rind and enough of the dressing to coat everything generously. Taste for seasoning and add sea salt and black pepper. Scatter with the remaining almonds, some shavings of Manchego or parmesan (if using), and serve drizzled with a fabulous extra virgin olive oil.

The sweet earthiness of beetroot is magnificent, especially when it's roasted with lots of salt and pepper – for me, it doesn't really need much else. But recently I got into the habit of using the leafy green tops as well, and discovered they're delicious reunited with the root in a buttery balsamic sauce. It's lovely simply served like this as a side to roast meat, and it's so adaptable. Glam it up with nuts or dukkah (the Middle Eastern spice blend made with toasted nuts and seeds) sprinkled over the top. To make it more substantial, dot the beetroot with goat's cheese or yoghurt, or serve it on a platter topped with toasted pistachios and a creamy orb of burrata cheese as I've done here.

Roast beetroot with beetroot greens and balsamic

Serves 4

6 raw beetroot, about tennis-
   ball sized
3 rosemary sprigs
1 tablespoon olive oil
sea salt flakes
freshly ground black pepper
30 g (1 oz) goat's butter (cow's
   milk butter is fine)
2 tablespoons white balsamic
   vinegar
30 ml (1 fl oz) balsamic vinegar
1 handful toasted pistachio
   nuts, chopped
200 g (7 oz) ball of burrata
   cheese

Preheat the oven to 220°C (425°F). Trim the beetroot, keeping about 2 handfuls of the beetroot greens. Wash, dry and cut the greens into wide slices. Set aside. Peel the beetroot and cut them into quarters. Put the beetroot in a roasting tin with the rosemary sprigs, drizzle with the olive oil and season with lots of sea salt and black pepper. Toss to coat the beetroot with oil. Cover with a double layer of foil and roast for about 40 minutes or until tender.

When the beetroot is cooked, melt the butter in a frying pan over medium–high heat. Add the beetroot and reserved beetroot greens to the foaming butter and toss to coat. Cook until the greens just start to wilt – you don't want them to turn limp and sludge-coloured. Add both the balsamic vinegars and stir around in the pan until the liquid almost all bubbles away. Check for seasoning and add more salt and pepper if necessary.

Serve immediately, scattered with the pistachios and topped with the burrata cheese.

This is one of the tastiest ways to cook vegetables and one of my favourite ways to eat them. The trick is to char the vegetables in a very hot chargrill pan until they have lovely stripes, but not to overcook or burn them: a barbecue is fantastic for this. You can cook the capsicum this way, too – but watch the heat, as you don't want to incinerate the sliced vegetables.

Charred vegetables with preserved lemon dressing

Serves 4–6 as a side

2 red capsicums (peppers)
2 yellow zucchini (courgettes), about 250 g (9 oz) each
olive oil, for brushing
8 young asparagus spears
2 little gem lettuces, quartered lengthways
1 handful basil leaves

For the dressing

2 large handfuls parsley, thick stalks removed, roughly chopped
3 tablespoons chopped preserved lemon rind, or to taste
2 garlic cloves, chopped
¼ teaspoon sea salt flakes
90 ml (3 fl oz) extra virgin olive oil
freshly ground black pepper

Preheat your grill (broiler) to its highest setting, then cook the whole capsicums until blackened and blistered all over. Place in a bowl, cover with plastic wrap and set aside. (This will make the skins easier to peel off.)

While this is happening, heat a chargrill pan until very hot, then slice the zucchini lengthways into 5 mm (¼ inch) strips. Brush with olive oil, then cook for 2 minutes on each side or until nicely striped. Transfer to a plate lined with paper towel to drain in a single layer.

Next, brush the asparagus and lettuces all over with olive oil and cook in batches until lightly charred – the asparagus should take about 4 minutes (depending on thickness) and the lettuce about 2 minutes on each side. You want the vegetables to retain a little bite and be lightly charred with nice stripes from the chargrill pan. Transfer to a plate lined with paper towel to drain in a single layer.

Peel the skins off the capsicums, remove the stalks and the seeds, and cut the flesh into wide strips – try to collect the juices. Arrange all the vegetables on a large serving platter.

Now, make the dressing. Gather the parsley, lemon rind, garlic and sea salt into a pile on your chopping board and chop together to produce a rough mixture. Scoop into a mixing bowl, stir in the extra virgin olive oil and any capsicum juices you managed to save, and season with black pepper. Have a taste and add more lemon rind, salt or pepper if you like.

Pour some of the dressing over the vegetables, tear the basil leaves and add these too, then lightly toss the mixture with your hands. Add more dressing, tossing after each addition, until everything is generously coated. Serve at room temperature.

Members of the onion family are so often used as flavour building blocks that it's easy to overlook their loveliness as stand-alone vegetables. Baked very slowly until meltingly soft and unctuous, these shallots are one of my favourite accompaniments to roast meat or juicy steaks. Yes, they take a long time to cook, but they attend to themselves in the oven for most of it, and your kitchen will be filled with the wonderful sweet roasting smell. Do keep an eye on them for the final half-hour after you increase the oven temperature, as you don't want them to burn.

Confit shallots with herbs and garlic

Serves 4–6 as a side

700 g (1 lb 9 oz) French shallots
90 ml (3 fl oz) olive oil
2 rosemary sprigs
2 oregano sprigs
3 bay leaves
8 garlic cloves
2 teaspoons fine sea salt
1 tablespoon white balsamic vinegar
a generous pinch of sugar

Preheat the oven to 140°C (275°F).

Peel the shallots, halving them if they are large. Warm the olive oil over medium heat in a large flameproof casserole dish. Add the shallots, herbs, peeled garlic cloves and sea salt, and stir to combine. Bring to a simmer, then add a splash of water and cover. Transfer to the oven and bake for 2 hours or so until very tender, stirring now and then so that all the shallots get a turn at the bottom of the dish.

Remove the dish from the oven and stir in the balsamic vinegar and sugar. Increase the oven to 180°C (350°F) and continue to cook, uncovered, for a further 30 minutes or until the shallots are very soft and starting to caramelise and most of the liquid has been cooked off. Serve warm or at room temperature.

I confess to gobbling up an entire batch of this in a single sitting – that's how much I love this colourful, flavour-packed dish. It's inspired by caponata, the traditional Sicilian stew that features capers (hence the name, I assume) and a mouth-tingling sweet and sour sauce. I've left out some traditional ingredients, like olives and celery, and added in my own. Eat the whole lot yourself like I did if you wish, but it's more commonly shared and served as a side.

Vibrant vegetable stew with capers

Serves 4 as a side

300 g (10½ oz) eggplant (aubergine)
1 teaspoon fine sea salt
90 ml (3 fl oz) olive oil
2 red onions, thinly sliced
2 garlic cloves, finely chopped
200 g (7 oz) ripe mixed tomatoes, diced
120 g (4¼ oz) mixed red and yellow capsicums (peppers), cut into 2 cm (¾ inch) pieces
1 teaspoon nigella seeds
1 tablespoon capers, rinsed
30 g (1 oz) sultanas (golden raisins)
a generous pinch of chilli flakes
2 tablespoons red wine vinegar
sea salt flakes
freshly ground black pepper
1 handful basil leaves, torn

Cut the eggplant into 2 cm (¾ inch) cubes. Place in a colander set over a bowl, sprinkle with the fine sea salt and toss well. Set aside to drain for 20 minutes. When the time is up, squeeze out any excess liquid and pat dry with paper towel.

While the eggplant is draining, heat 30 ml (1 fl oz) of the olive oil in a frying pan and fry the onions until soft, about 8 minutes. Add the chopped garlic and fry for 2 minutes more, then transfer the mixture to a plate. Wipe out the frying pan and add the remaining olive oil. Warm over medium–high heat and fry the eggplant until golden and crisp, about 5–10 minutes.

Return the onion and garlic to the pan and add the tomatoes, capsicums, nigella seeds and 125 ml (4 fl oz/½ cup) water. Gently simmer over medium–low heat for 15 minutes or until you have lovely stewed vegetables in a rich sauce, with the capsicums still retaining a little bite.

Pull the pan off the heat, add the remaining ingredients and stir well to combine. Taste for seasoning and adjust with extra salt or pepper if needed. Serve warm or cold.

Leafy greens

In my parallel life, I source all my leafy greens the traditional Mediterranean way by scrambling up a hillside to pick them wild and fresh. Back in reality, like most of us, I don't have this romantic option. But it still is possible to prepare leafy greens in a way that retains the essence of Mediterranean cooking.

Traditional wild greens include nettles, wild fennel, dandelion, mallow, wild spinach and amaranth, along with dozens of others. Fortunately, these are interchangeable with greens readily available to most of us, including silverbeet (Swiss chard), cavolo nero and other types of kale, Asian vegetables, English spinach, collard greens, spring greens, watercress, rocket (arugula) and herbs. Don't forget the green tops of beetroot and turnips are also edible and delicious. And always buy what's in season.

Every country in the Mediterranean has its own way of cooking leafy greens, but the Greek dish *horta* is the most famous. I cook mine with lemon-infused olive oil, which is really simple to make and useful to have to hand. Just pour 200 ml (7 fl oz) of extra virgin olive oil into a saucepan, add strips of zest from two lemons and heat gently until you see tiny champagne bubbles form. Remove the pan from the heat and leave the oil to infuse for 30 minutes, then discard the lemon zest and store the infused oil in a screw-top jar.

For the greens, simply cook them in boiling salted water until just tender (don't overcook them!) then drain well and squeeze out any excess water. Warm a glug of your lemon-infused oil in a frying pan, add the greens and a clove of crushed garlic if you like, and cook, stirring, until the leaves are hot and coated in a slick of oil. Add lots of salt and pepper, and some briny feta cheese or pine nuts if you wish, before serving warm or at room temperature.

I hesitated before including this recipe – it shrieks 1970s dinner parties, doesn't it? But it's such a delicious dish, still enjoyed in various guises all over the Mediterranean, that it had to go in. There might be a lot of rice left over here – the amount you need obviously depends on the size of the tomatoes. Just serve any extra rice alongside the tomatoes.

Retro tomatoes stuffed with spicy saffron rice and herbs

Serves 4 as a side

4 large ripe but firm tomatoes
sea salt flakes
100 g (3½ oz/½ cup) long-grain white rice, rinsed well and drained
a generous pinch of saffron threads, chopped
2 tablespoons olive oil, plus extra for drizzling
1 onion, finely chopped
2 garlic cloves, finely chopped
1–3 teaspoons harissa paste, or to taste
1 tablespoon pine nuts, toasted
about 10 mint leaves, chopped
1 small handful flat-leaf parsley leaves, chopped
1 small handful oregano leaves, chopped
freshly ground black pepper

Cut the tops off the tomatoes and remove the flesh and cores with a melon baller or teaspoon – try not to pierce the skins. Season the insides well with sea salt and set the tomatoes upside down on a wire rack or paper towel to drain a little, alongside the lids. Chop the tomato flesh, put it into a sieve set over a bowl and press down with the back of a spoon to collect the pulpy juices. Discard what remains in the sieve and set the juices to one side.

Put the rice in a saucepan with the saffron and a pinch of sea salt, and cover with 225 ml (7½ fl oz) water. Bring to the boil, then reduce the heat to low and cover. Gently simmer for 15 minutes or until the rice is tender and the water is absorbed. Fluff the rice with a fork and set aside.

Preheat the oven to 180°C (350°F) and lightly oil an ovenproof dish that will fit the tomatoes snugly.

Heat 1 tablespoon of the olive oil in a frying pan and fry the onion over medium heat until very soft, about 8 minutes. Add the garlic and harissa paste and stir for a couple of minutes. Pull the pan off the heat and add the cooked rice, pine nuts, reserved tomato juices and remaining olive oil. Mix in the herbs and season to taste with sea salt and black pepper.

Fill the tomatoes with the rice mixture, pressing down with the back of a spoon to squeeze in as much as possible. Pop the tops back on and transfer the tomatoes to the prepared dish. Drizzle with olive oil and bake for 40 minutes or until the tomatoes are beautifully soft – almost collapsing – and oozing juices.

A real celebration of tender young vegetables, this is springtime in a pan and I love it. I know it seems like a palaver to pod fresh broad beans and peas, but I don't intend this as a quick weeknight dinner: it's a celebratory dish. Be careful not to overcook the vegetables – they should still be a little al dente.

Braised peas, broad beans and asparagus with tarragon, mint and shallots

Serves 4 as a side

200 g (7 oz) podded broad beans
2 tablespoons olive oil
4 French shallots, quartered lengthways
sea salt flakes
8 young asparagus spears, cut into 4 cm (1½ inch) pieces
200 g (7 oz/1¼ cups) shelled peas
185 ml (6 fl oz/¾ cup) warm chicken or vegetable stock
finely grated zest and juice of ½ lemon, or to taste
1 handful tarragon leaves, chopped
1 handful mint leaves, chopped
freshly ground black pepper

First, blanch the broad beans in boiling water for 1 minute, then plunge them into cold water. The skins should slip off quite easily to reveal their vibrant shiny green colour. Set aside.

Heat the olive oil in a large frying pan and fry the shallots with a pinch of sea salt over medium heat for a few minutes until they are starting to soften. Add the asparagus and peas, and toss to coat in the oil. Cook over medium–high heat for 3 minutes, shaking the pan frequently, then add the broad beans and cook for a further minute.

Pour in the stock, reduce the heat and simmer for a few minutes or until the vegetables are just tender but still retain some bite, and the stock is almost all absorbed. Add a splash of warm water if the vegetables aren't cooked by the time the stock evaporates.

When the vegetables are done, stir in the lemon zest, lemon juice and herbs, then taste to see if you need more sea salt, black pepper or lemon juice. Serve warm.

Romesco is a very more-ish, slightly sweet, slightly tart Catalan sauce that's delicious with just about everything, especially grilled fish, chicken or vegetables. It's also a tasty way to nudge more nuts into your diet. Serve this as a side dish at a barbecue – make the sauce ahead and just cook the vegetables when you are ready to eat: they take only moments. If you have any sauce left over, just pop it into a jar and keep it in the fridge to dollop on leftovers later.

Charred spring onions, leeks and asparagus with romesco sauce

Serves 4 as a side

500 g (1 lb 2 oz) mix of large spring onions (scallions), baby leeks and thin asparagus spears
extra virgin olive oil, for brushing

For the romesco sauce

80 g (2¾ oz/½ cup) blanched almonds
40 g (1½ oz/¼ cup) skinless hazelnuts
2 tomatoes, halved
2 medium red chillies, halved lengthways, seeds removed
230 ml (7¾ fl oz) extra virgin olive oil, or to taste
30 g (1 oz/½ cup) fresh breadcrumbs
4 garlic cloves, crushed
2 teaspoons smoked paprika
60 g (2¼ oz) roasted red capsicums (peppers) in oil, drained weight
a generous pinch of chilli flakes
1 tablespoon red wine vinegar, or to taste
sea salt flakes
freshly ground black pepper

Start by making the romesco sauce. Preheat the oven to 180°C (350°F). Spread the nuts out on a baking tray with a rim. Put the tomatoes and chillies in a small roasting tin and drizzle with 1 tablespoon of the olive oil. Put the nuts on the top oven rack and the tomatoes and chillies on the bottom rack. Roast for 8 minutes or until the nuts are golden. Remove the nuts from the oven and set aside to cool, then transfer the tomatoes and chillies to the top rack. Cook for a further 10 minutes or until soft and bubbling. Set aside to cool a little.

While this is happening, heat 2 tablespoons of the olive oil in a frying pan, add the breadcrumbs and fry over medium–high heat, stirring often, until the crumbs smell fragrant and start to turn golden. Add the garlic and paprika, and fry for a couple of minutes more – be careful not to burn the mixture.

When everything is cooked, put the nuts, tomatoes, chillies, capsicums, chilli flakes, red wine vinegar and the breadcrumb mixture in a food processor. Pulse until you produce a chunky paste. Scrape the paste into a bowl, then gradually stir in the remaining olive oil. Have a taste and add sea salt, black pepper and more vinegar or oil if you think it needs it. Add a splash of water if the mixture is very thick. Set to one side.

Heat a chargrill pan until very hot or heat the barbecue grill. Lightly brush the vegetables with olive oil and cook, turning now and then, until tender and charred with stripes.

Pile the vegetables onto a serving plate and spoon some of the sauce over the top with the rest served alongside for guests to help themselves.

This wonderful dish is like the love child of two classics: Spain's *patatas bravas* and Greece's potato and tomato stew. It's rich and hearty, and lovely served with roast meat.

Potatoes in paprika-spiked sauce

Serves 6–8 as a side

1 kg (2 lb 4 oz) boiling potatoes
2 tablespoons olive oil
1 large onion, finely chopped
150 g (5½ oz) roasted red
    capsicums (peppers) in oil
    (drained weight), chopped
2 garlic cloves, finely chopped
500 ml (17 fl oz/2 cups)
    tomato passata
a large pinch of caster
    (superfine) sugar
1 tablespoon sweet smoked
    paprika
½ teaspoon Aleppo pepper
    or cayenne pepper
2 bay leaves
sea salt flakes
freshly ground black pepper

Start by preheating the oven to 180°C (350°F), then prepare the potatoes. Peel and cut them into 5 mm (¼ inch) slices and par-boil in salted water for 5 minutes – it's important that you don't overcook them or they will disintegrate. Drain and leave in a colander set over the pan so they dry out a little.

Meanwhile, heat the olive oil in a saucepan and gently fry the onion and capsicums over low heat for 10 minutes or until very soft. Add the garlic and cook for a few minutes more. Add the passata, sugar, paprika, Aleppo pepper or cayenne pepper, bay leaves and 200 ml (7 fl oz) water and stir to combine. Season with sea salt and black pepper and simmer until the sauce has thickened a little, about 10 minutes.

Arrange half the potato slices in a small ovenproof dish – 30 x 18 cm (12 x 7 inches) is perfect – and ladle half the sauce over them, making sure you cover all the potatoes. Repeat the layering with the rest of the potatoes and sauce. Tightly cover with foil. Bake for 30 minutes or until the potatoes are tender and cooked right through.

Carrots are a Mediterranean staple and this is a gorgeous way to eat them, as their honeyed sweetness plays beautifully with the lemony sharpness of the dressing. To make the most delicious sauce you need to use lush green carrot tops, not manky brown ones. We often eat these as a side to Roast butterflied chicken with herbs and potatoes (page 104) because the green sauce is lovely with poultry. The carrots also go well with a side of spelt or other grains.

Honeyed roasted carrots with carrot top dressing

Serves 4 as a side

100 ml (3½ fl oz) olive oil
2 tablespoons honey
1 heaped teaspoon za'atar
1 teaspoon ground cumin
sea salt flakes
freshly ground black pepper
1 bunch carrots with the green
    tops attached, about 500 g
    (1 lb 2 oz)
1 garlic clove
2 tablespoons lemon juice

Preheat the oven to 200°C (400°F). Whisk together 30 ml (1 fl oz) of the oil, the honey, za'atar, cumin and some sea salt and black pepper. Chop the green tops off the carrots, leaving a little bit of stalk on, and set aside. Put the carrots in a roasting tin and toss with the honeyed oil mixture. Roast for 30–40 minutes or until the carrots are tender and starting to caramelise.

Meanwhile, roughly chop enough of the leaves from the carrot tops to make a handful and pop them in a food processor. Add the remaining oil, the garlic and lemon juice, and season with sea salt. Blitz to make a smooth sauce.

When the carrots are done, drizzle with some of the sauce and serve the rest on the side.

Almond butter adds a rich creaminess to the dressing of this unconventional potato salad. I love the contrast with the salty samphire and zingy lemon juice. Use shop-bought almond butter if you like, but it's easy to make. Just tip a cup of lightly toasted almonds into a food processor – skins on or off, whichever you prefer – and blitz for up to 20 minutes, scraping down the side of the bowl now and then. You might think it's never going to work, but if you stick with it the nuts eventually release their oil to form a delicious smooth paste. This is perfect as a side to white fish.

Warm potato salad with samphire and almond butter dressing

Serves 4 as a side

800 g (1 lb 12 oz) Jersey royal potatoes or other small boiling potatoes
60 g (2¼ oz) samphire
1 handful basil leaves, torn

For the dressing

2 tablespoons almond butter
1 garlic clove, crushed
2 tablespoons olive oil
75 ml (2¼ fl oz) lemon juice, or to taste
sea salt flakes
freshly ground black pepper

Cook the potatoes in boiling salted water for about 25 minutes or until tender. Leave the skins on as they add lots of flavour. While the potatoes are cooking, blanch the samphire in boiling water, then drain well.

Make the dressing before the potatoes are cooked: put the almond butter, garlic, olive oil, lemon juice, sea salt and black pepper in a screw-top jar. Shake vigorously to make a smooth dressing, adding a splash of warm water to loosen it if necessary. Have a taste and add more lemon juice or salt and pepper if necessary.

When the potatoes are cooked, drain, then halve the smaller ones and quarter the large ones, and pop them in a salad bowl. Add the samphire and most of the torn basil and gently toss with enough of the dressing to generously coat the potatoes. Serve with the remaining basil on top.

Kale coated with oil and cooked in a dry frying pan takes on a deliciously smoky flavour, and the leaves turn charred and crisp in parts and tender in others. It's wonderful. A dish I ate at Gjelina, a fantastic modern Italian restaurant in Los Angeles, inspired this recipe – Californians sure do love their kale! After you add the dressing, get in there and toss it with your hands so all the leaves get a good coating.

Kale with garlicky lime yoghurt and almonds

Serves 2–4 as a side

300 g (10½ oz) cavolo nero (Tuscan kale) or other non-curly kale
2 tablespoons olive oil
¼ teaspoon sea salt flakes
50 g (1¾ oz) blanched almonds, lightly toasted and roughly chopped

For the dressing

120 g (4¼ oz) Greek-style yoghurt
2 tablespoons olive oil
2 tablespoons lime juice, or to taste
½ French shallot, finely chopped
1 small garlic clove, finely chopped
a few mint leaves, finely chopped
sea salt flakes
freshly ground black pepper

First, make the dressing so the flavours have time to mingle. Put all the ingredients in a screw-top jar and shake well. Set aside.

Now, prepare the kale. Slice the leaves in half lengthways and trim away the tough central stalk. Depending on the size of the leaves, you might have to cut them in half crossways to fit into your frying pan. Combine the olive oil and sea salt in a little bowl. Lightly brush both sides of the leaves with the oil and massage with your hands to make sure they are evenly coated.

Heat a chargrill pan or large frying pan until very hot and add the kale leaves in a single layer (do this in batches). Cook both sides until they are nicely charred in patches and crisp at the edges but not burnt – this should take about 30–60 seconds for each side.

Tear or cut the kale leaves into large bite-sized pieces, pop them into a salad bowl with most of the almonds and toss with enough of the dressing to coat. Sprinkle over the remaining almonds and serve immediately.

Lime and pumpkin might not seem like obvious partners but the sharp and spicy citrus really brightens up the earthy sweetness of my favourite roast vegetable. The yoghurt dressing also elevates this dish to something more than a side – we could happily eat it as a main course at our house, with perhaps another vegetable dish or salad.

Lime and honey roasted pumpkin with mint yoghurt and pepitas

Serves 4 as a side

800 g (1 lb 12 oz) butternut pumpkin (squash), halved and cut into 1 cm (½ inch) slices (leave the skin on or take it off if you prefer)
1 tablespoon olive oil
1 tablespoon lime juice
finely grated zest of ½ lime
1 teaspoon honey
a generous pinch of Aleppo pepper
1 tablespoon pepitas (pumpkin seeds), lightly toasted

For the mint yoghurt

3 tablespoons Greek-style yoghurt
2 tablespoons finely chopped mint leaves
1 teaspoon olive oil
1 small garlic clove, crushed

Preheat the oven to 220°C (425°F). Arrange the pumpkin in a single layer in a roasting tin. Whisk together the olive oil, lime juice, lime zest, honey and Aleppo pepper. Drizzle this mixture over the pumpkin and toss so it's all nicely coated. Roast for 30–35 minutes or until the pumpkin is tender and a little charred.

Meanwhile, stir together the mint yoghurt ingredients and set to one side so the flavours can mingle.

To serve, transfer the pumpkin to a serving plate, drizzle with the mint yoghurt and scatter with the pepitas. Serve immediately.

Witlof deserves a bit more love, in my opinion – I assume it's the bitterness that puts people off. Cooked like this, however, the leaves lose some of that sharpness and take on a lovely smokiness. Paired with the apples and thyme, they make a beautiful dish, perfect for autumn and winter when a little vibrant crunch is needed to freshen up warming comfort food.

Chargrilled witlof with sautéed apples and walnuts

Serves 4 as a side

4 firm heads red witlof (chicory),
   quartered lengthways
1 tablespoon olive oil, plus extra
   for brushing
2 large red apples
1 tablespoon finely chopped
   thyme leaves, plus extra
   sprigs to serve
1 teaspoon honey
30 g (1 oz/¼ cup) walnuts,
   lightly toasted and chopped

For the dressing

3 tablespoons apple juice
3 tablespoons olive oil
1 tablespoon lemon juice
sea salt flakes
freshly ground black pepper

First, make the dressing. Put the ingredients in a screw-top jar and shake well. Set aside to use later.

Now, heat a chargrill pan until very hot, brush the witlof with olive oil and cook until charred with stripes all over. Reduce the heat to low and set the pan half on and half off the heat to keep warm.

Quarter and core the apples (leave the skin on for lovely colour), then cut into slices about 3–5 mm (⅛–¼ inch) thick at the widest part. Heat the 1 tablespoon olive oil in a frying pan, add the apples and thyme, and cook, turning the apples occasionally, for a couple of minutes. Add the honey and continue cooking until the apples turn slightly golden but still retain a little bite.

Transfer the witlof and apples to a serving plate, add the walnuts and gently toss with enough of the dressing to generously coat. Serve immediately, topped with thyme sprigs.

Sweet things

There's nothing more satisfying than a greedy slice of squidgy, salt-crusted, herb-strewn, garlicky focaccia, except perhaps this sweet version of the classic Italian flatbread. It's not overly sugary – just some fruit and fruit juice – but it satisfies a sweet craving in a most delicious way. Raspberries are lovely, but red grapes or other chopped fruit also work well.

Raspberry focaccia

Serves 6–8

2 teaspoons instant dried yeast
1 teaspoon honey
300 ml (10½ fl oz) warm water
400 g (14 oz) strong flour,
    plus extra for dusting
100 g (3½ oz) fine semolina
2 teaspoons fennel seeds
a pinch of fine sea salt
olive oil, for oiling and drizzling
250 ml (9 fl oz/1 cup)
    unsweetened red grape or
    pomegranate juice
about 200 g (7 oz) raspberries
1 handful slivered almonds

Start by mixing the yeast and honey into the warm water and set aside for 5 minutes to froth.

While this is happening, whisk together the flour, semolina, fennel seeds and sea salt. Make a well in the centre of the dry ingredients and then slowly pour in the yeasty water, mixing as you go to make a shaggy dough. Bring the dough together into a ball, tip out onto an oiled work surface and knead for 10–15 minutes or until smooth and elastic. Alternatively, transfer the dough to an electric mixer with a dough hook attachment and mix for 10 minutes. Put the dough in an oiled bowl, cover with plastic wrap and set aside somewhere warm for about 1 hour or until doubled in size.

Meanwhile, simmer the fruit juice in a small saucepan until reduced to about 3 tablespoons, then set to one side to cool.

Preheat the oven to 220°C (425°F). Lightly oil a 20 x 30 cm (8 x 12 inch) shallow baking tray.

Punch down the dough, tip it into the baking tray and gently flatten it into the corners. Make dimples in the top with your fingertips and push the raspberries deep into the holes. Drizzle with the reduced juice, sprinkle with the almonds and about 1 tablespoon of the olive oil. Cover with a clean tea towel and set aside somewhere warm for 20 minutes.

Bake the focaccia for 20 minutes or until golden and cooked through. Leave to cool on a wire rack for 15 minutes before serving.

This insanely pretty dessert is based on 'spoon sweets' – fruit preserved in sugar syrup and traditionally served on little spoons alongside coffee at the end of a meal. They're intensely sweet mouthfuls, hugely popular throughout Greece and the eastern Mediterranean, and the flavours vary according to the seasons. I first made this at the home of a friend who grows plums and lavender in her garden. I thought that combining the two would be wonderful – and it is. A note: there is a lot of sugar in this recipe, but don't worry too much as the portions are intended to be very small.

Sticky plum and lavender compote

Serves 6–8

8 ripe but firm yellow-fleshed plums, about 450 g (1 lb)
200 g (7 oz) caster (superfine) sugar
½ teaspoon dried lavender buds
1 tablespoon lemon juice
1 strip lemon zest
Greek-style yoghurt, to serve

Halve and stone the plums and place in a mixing bowl. Gradually sprinkle with the sugar and lavender, gently tossing as you go so all the fruit is coated. Set aside overnight to allow the plums to release their juices, stirring now and then to help the sugar dissolve.

Tip the plums and all of the juices into a saucepan. Stir to dissolve any remaining sugar crystals. Add 3 tablespoons water and cook over medium heat for 5 minutes or until the plums are just tender but still hold their shape easily. The skins will start to loosen from the fruit, but don't worry as they add gorgeous colour and taste tender and delicious. Remove the plums from the syrup with a slotted spoon and put to one side in a bowl.

Add the lemon juice and lemon zest to the syrup. Simmer until the syrup reaches 120°C (235°F) on a sugar thermometer, or until it coats the back of a spoon. Take the pan off the heat, add the plums and gently stir until they are coated in syrup.

Serve the plums and the syrup at room temperature with very cold Greek-style yoghurt.

Moist, lemony and adorned with juicy figs, this cake is simple, lovely and a breeze to make. It's not health food per se, but is reasonably low in sugar and contains no dairy or wheat. Try to use a mild-flavoured olive oil or its flavour might shine through too strongly. The cake tastes fabulous (and perhaps better) the day after it's made, if it lasts that long.

Fig and lemon polenta squares

Makes 16 squares

200 g (7 oz/2 cups) almond meal
130 g (4½ oz/⅔ cup) fine polenta
1 teaspoon baking powder
a pinch of fine sea salt
130 ml (4 fl oz) light-flavoured olive oil
125 g (4½ oz) caster (superfine) sugar
finely grated zest and juice of 2 lemons
3 tablespoons orange blossom honey or other floral honey
3 large eggs, lightly beaten
8 large ripe figs, halved lengthways

Preheat the oven to 160°C (315°F). Oil a 20 cm (8 inch) square cake tin and line the tin with baking paper, allowing it to overhang the edges. If you scrunch up the baking paper before you line the tin, the paper will stick and fit easily.

In a mixing bowl, whisk together the almond meal, polenta, baking powder and sea salt. Using an electric mixer or a whisk and a strong arm, beat together the olive oil, sugar, lemon zest, lemon juice and honey until well combined. Gradually beat in the eggs so the mixture is creamy and frothy.

Stir the egg mixture into the dry ingredients until well combined. Don't worry about the batter being thin – it's meant to be like that. Pour into the prepared tin and press the figs, skin side up, into the batter in four rows of four.

Bake the cake for about 40 minutes or until a skewer comes out clean. Leave to cool in the tin for 10 minutes and then lift out using the baking paper handles. Cut the cake into 16 squares so that each piece is adorned with a fig.

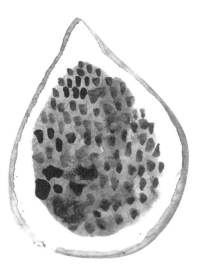

Salty. Sweet. Soft. Crunchy. Plus syrup. What more could you want from a dessert? The flavours here might seem a bit unlikely, but the combination is delicious. The distinctive liquorice taste of aniseed, a flavour widely used in the Mediterranean, works especially well with the date syrup.

Baked feta parcels with warm date syrup and walnuts

Serves 4

200 g (7 oz) block feta cheese
4 sheets filo pastry, about
    30 x 38 cm (12 x 15 inches),
    chilled until needed
3 tablespoons olive oil
1 teaspoon chopped thyme
    leaves
grated zest of 1 lemon
½ teaspoon aniseeds
2 teaspoons honey
90 ml (3 fl oz) date syrup
40 g (1½ oz/⅓ cup) walnuts,
    lightly toasted and roughly
    chopped

Preheat the oven to 180°C (350°F) and line a large baking tray with baking paper.

Slice the block of feta in half horizontally to make two large thin rectangles, then cut the rectangles in half crossways to make two small thin rectangles. Put to one side.

Put a sheet of filo on your work surface with the short side closest to you (keep the other sheets between two damp tea towels) and brush the top half with olive oil. Fold the sheet in half, then brush with more oil. Place a rectangle of feta close to the middle of the shortest edge, sprinkle over one-quarter each of the thyme, lemon zest, aniseeds and honey, then fold the sides of the filo inwards. Brush a little more oil over the filo and roll up, brushing the top of the filo as you go. Transfer to the prepared tray and repeat to make four parcels in total.

Bake the feta parcels for 20–25 minutes or until golden and the feta is very soft.

While this is happening, gently warm the date syrup in a small saucepan, but don't let it boil – you just want it slightly warmed.

Serve the parcels straight from the oven with the date syrup spooned over the top and scattered with the walnuts.

A fluffy Victoria sponge this is not, rather it is a dense and flavourful cake that carries just a little crunch from the semolina. It's my favourite kind of cake. Served warm, with a little yoghurt or mascarpone cheese, it makes a lovely dessert. But cold the next day (when I think the flavour improves) it's fantastic with a cup of tea.

Orange, thyme and semolina cake

Makes a 20 cm (8 inch) cake

grated zest of 1 orange plus the
    juice of ½ orange
125 ml (4 fl oz/½ cup) olive oil
2 teaspoons orange blossom
    water
160 g (5½ oz) fine semolina
2 tablespoons plain (all-
    purpose) flour
3 tablespoons almond meal
1 teaspoon baking powder
3 eggs
150 g (5½ oz/⅔ cup) golden
    caster (superfine) sugar
2 tablespoons chopped
    pistachio nuts

For the syrup

120 g (4¼ oz) caster (superfine)
    sugar
300 ml (10½ fl oz) orange juice
finely grated zest of 1 orange
1 thyme sprig

Preheat the oven to 180°C (350°F). Line a 20 cm (8 inch) square cake tin with baking paper or foil, letting it overhang the edges.

Combine the orange zest and juice, olive oil and orange blossom water in a bowl, stir and set aside. Whisk together the semolina, flour, almond meal and baking powder and set aside.

Use an electric mixer to beat the eggs with the sugar until pale, thick and creamy. Stir the semolina mixture into the egg mixture, alternating with the orange juice mixture. Pour into the tin and bake for 25–30 minutes or until a skewer comes out clean.

While the cake is cooking, put all the ingredients for the syrup in a small saucepan and stir until it comes to the boil. Reduce the heat and gently simmer for 15 minutes. Pull the pan off the heat and set aside to cool.

While the cake is still hot, use a skewer to poke lots of holes in the top. Remove the thyme sprig from the syrup and pour the syrup over the cake, encouraging it into the holes. Scatter with the pistachios, cut into squares and serve warm or cold.

This is one of my family's favourite tarts. There's something about the fusion of peach and rosemary, and the almond meal in the crust, that makes it especially summery and delicious. Once, when I was testing this out of season, I resorted to using hard peaches and the result was terrible. You need ripe ones for this as their lovely sweet juices form the filling.

Peach and rosemary galette with an almond crust

Serves 6–8

8 ripe peaches, about 900 g (2 lb) in total
50 g (1¾ oz) caster (superfine) sugar
1 tablespoon cornflour (cornstarch)
2 teaspoons finely chopped rosemary leaves, plus extra leaves for sprinkling
2 tablespoons peach or apricot jam, warmed
2 tablespoons almond meal
1 egg, lightly beaten
Greek-style yoghurt or mascarpone cheese, to serve

For the pastry

200 g (7 oz/1⅓ cups) plain (all-purpose) flour, plus extra for rolling
60 g (2¼ oz) caster (superfine) sugar
50 g (1¾ oz/½ cup) almond meal
½ teaspoon ground cinnamon
a pinch of salt
125 g (4½ oz) cold butter
2 egg yolks, lightly beaten
2–3 tablespoons iced water

First, make the pastry. Whisk together the flour, sugar, almond meal, cinnamon and salt in a mixing bowl. Using the largest holes of a box grater, grate the butter into the flour mixture. Mix with a butter knife until you have lots of tiny bits of butter coated in flour. Add the egg yolks and mix these in with the knife, then gradually mix in enough of the iced water to make a dough that comes together into a ball without crumbling. Turn out onto a lightly floured work surface and briefly knead, then shape into a disc. Wrap in plastic wrap and chill for 30 minutes.

While the dough is chilling, halve, stone and thinly slice the peaches, leaving the skin on as it adds lovely colour. Place in a mixing bowl, sprinkle with the sugar, cornflour and rosemary and gently toss so the peaches are coated. Set aside until the dough is ready to use.

When you take the dough out of the fridge, preheat the oven to 190°C (375°F) and place a large baking tray inside.

Roll out the dough between two sheets of lightly floured baking paper to make a 35 cm (14 inch) circle. Carefully peel back the top layer of paper. Stir the warmed jam to loosen it, then spoon some into the centre of the dough and spread out with the back of a spoon, leaving a 4 cm (1½ inch) border. Add just enough jam to make a thin layer. Sprinkle with the almond meal, then arrange the peaches on top in an even layer – don't add too much of the juice left in the bowl or the pastry will turn soggy.

Fold the pastry border inwards, pleating and gently pressing to form a neat edge, and brush the border with the egg. Quickly remove the baking tray from the oven, slide the galette and baking paper onto the tray and bake for 30–35 minutes or until the pastry is golden on top and underneath.

Serve the galette warm, sprinkled with rosemary leaves, with a good dollop of Greek-style yoghurt or mascarpone cheese.

Fruit

In Mediterranean countries, plates of sun-kissed fruit serve as bookends to the day. Finely sliced citrus sprinkled with spice might make a fresh and cooling breakfast, while a clutch of purple figs often crowns the evening meal. Of course, fruit is also nibbled on and strewn in sweet and savoury dishes throughout the day. Citrus, stone fruit, berries, apples, pears, figs, dates and pomegranates are among the favourites on the Mediterranean table, and readily available outside the region, too.

It goes without saying that perfectly fresh ripe fruit is best eaten raw. But even fruit-lovers sometimes need enticement to eat as much as they should, especially when produce isn't in its prime. That's certainly the case in my house and why I'm constantly chopping and peeling fruit destined for the pot or roasting tray. Stewed, sautéed or baked with spices – and maybe a splash of booze – cooking fruit can coax flavour from even the most insipid specimens. I honestly rank roast apples, pears or quince topped with rich Greek yoghurt (spiked with honey, rosewater or other aromatics) as a superlative dessert.

The tradition of enhancing savoury dishes with fruit came from the Moors and has been used in Mediterranean cooking ever since. And it's a very good thing. Dates, melted into slow-cooked meaty stews, add richness and extra depth of flavour. Pomegranate seeds, scattered over salads or even soups, add a satisfying tangy pop of flavour. Slices of sweet pear added to salads are a pleasing counterpoint to bitter leaves and tangy dressings. The list goes on.

I drink bucketfuls of chamomile tea each day and olive oil cakes are my favourite treat, so this is my idea of a perfect afternoon tea. Use chamomile flowers if you can. They're widely available these days and their flavour is intense, almost tangy, but tea bags also work nicely. I normally love the flavour of olive oil in cakes, but I've suggested using a mild version in this one so the chamomile can shine through.

Chamomile and honey olive oil cake

Makes a 20 cm (8 inch) cake

125 ml (4 fl oz/½ cup) milk, plus extra if needed

3 tablespoons chamomile flowers or 4 chamomile tea bags

250 g (9 oz/1⅔ cups) self-raising flour

150 g (5½ oz/⅔ cup) caster (superfine) sugar

1 teaspoon baking powder

a generous pinch of salt

250 ml (9 fl oz/1 cup) mild olive oil

70 g (2½ oz) honey

3 eggs

For the lemon icing

150 g (5½ oz) icing (confectioners') sugar, sifted

finely grated zest and juice of 1 lemon

a splash of milk

Preheat the oven to 160°C (315°F). Oil a 20 cm (8 inch) round cake tin and line the base with baking paper.

Pour the milk into a small saucepan and gently warm through without letting it reach the boil, then remove from the heat and add the chamomile flowers or tea bags. Set to one side for a good 10 minutes so the milk and chamomile can infuse and cool.

Now, whisk together the flour, sugar, baking powder and salt in a large bowl. In a separate bowl, whisk together the olive oil, honey and eggs.

Strain the chamomile flowers from the cooled milk, or remove the tea bags, and measure how much milk you have – you need 125 ml (4 fl oz/½ cup), so add more milk if necessary. Stir the infused milk into the oil mixture. Pour this mixture into the flour mixture, mixing until well combined and lump-free, but don't overbeat it.

Pour the batter into the tin and bake for 40–50 minutes or until the cake is golden and a skewer comes out almost clean. Leave the cake in the tin for 5 minutes, then turn out onto a wire rack to cool.

While the cake is cooking, stir together the lemon icing ingredients, keeping some of the lemon zest for the top of the cake and adding just enough milk to give it a loose pouring consistency.

When the cake is completely cold, drizzle with the lemon icing and sprinkle with the reserved lemon zest.

Carob reminds me of my childhood when my mother, a health food fanatic ahead of her time, fed it to us as a chocolate substitute. I didn't like it much back then, but now I love the flavour, having eaten it in Portugal and other parts of the Mediterranean where it's grown and widely used in baking and desserts. It's naturally sweeter than cocoa and contains less fat, more fibre and is loaded with calcium, so it's pretty good for you. But all that aside, this cake is lush – the juicy figs, rich carob notes and hazelnuts are a heavenly combination. Carob powder, also known as carob flour, is widely available online and in health food stores, but you can substitute it with 2 tablespoons of cocoa powder if you can't find it.

Fig, hazelnut and carob crumble cake

Makes a 23 cm (9 inch) cake

100 g (3½ oz/⅔ cup) skinless hazelnuts
140 g (5 oz) plain (all-purpose) flour
3 tablespoons carob powder
2 teaspoons baking powder
a pinch of fine sea salt
125 g (4½ oz) unsalted butter, softened
160 g (5½ oz) caster (superfine) sugar
2 large eggs, lightly beaten
75 ml (2¼ fl oz) milk
6–8 figs, quartered

For the crumble

100 g (3½ oz/⅔ cup) spelt flour or wholemeal plain flour (whole-wheat all-purpose flour)
60 g (2¼ oz) light brown sugar
60 g (2¼ oz) unsalted butter
½ teaspoon ground cinnamon

Preheat the oven to 170°C (325°F). Grease a 23 cm (9 inch) round spring-form cake tin and line the base with baking paper.

Tip the hazelnuts into a dry frying pan and toast over medium–high heat, shaking frequently, until fragrant and starting to turn golden. Tip into a food processor, then leave to cool for 5 minutes.

While this is happening, make the crumble mixture. Put the flour, brown sugar, butter and cinnamon in a small mixing bowl. Rub the butter into the dry ingredients with your fingertips until the mixture resembles coarse breadcrumbs. Set to one side.

Now, blitz the hazelnuts until finely ground. Tip into a mixing bowl and add the flour, carob powder, baking powder and sea salt. Whisk together, then put to one side.

Use an electric mixer or a wooden spoon to beat the butter and caster sugar together until pale and creamy. Add the eggs, little by little, beating well after each addition, until completely combined. Gradually stir the flour mixture into the butter mixture, alternating with the milk, until creamy and well combined.

Scrape the mixture into the tin and smooth the surface with a spatula. Press the fig quarters into the batter, cut side up, around the side of the tin, as well as one or two in the centre if there's room. Sprinkle the crumble mixture over the top. Bake for about 40–45 minutes or until a skewer comes out clean. Leave to cool in the tin for 10 minutes before releasing.

This Greek classic (with a few of my own variations) is pretty hard to beat when a rib-sticking pudding is called for. It's also perfect for those who believe life's too short to brush sheets of filo with melted butter – there's none of that involved here, just cutting it into pretty ribbons. I adore the slight bitterness of the marmalade but this works equally well if you leave it out.

Pomegranate, orange and marmalade filo pudding cake

Serves 8 generously

350 g (12 oz) filo pastry
150 ml (5 fl oz) olive oil, plus extra for brushing
1 blood orange
4 eggs
80 g (2¾ oz) caster (superfine) sugar
200 g (7 oz/¾ cup) Greek-style yoghurt, plus extra to serve
125 ml (4 fl oz/½ cup) freshly squeezed pomegranate juice (1 large or 2 small pomegranates)
2 teaspoons baking powder

For the syrup

125 ml (4 fl oz/½ cup) freshly squeezed pomegranate juice (1 large or 2 small pomegranates)
125 ml (4 fl oz/½ cup) freshly squeezed blood orange juice (about 1 large orange), skin reserved
2 tablespoons orange marmalade
150 g (5½ oz/⅔ cup) caster (superfine) sugar
½ cinnamon stick

Using kitchen scissors, cut the filo sheets into ribbons 2 cm (¾ inch) wide – you don't have to be precise. Loosen the ribbons with your fingers to separate, then spread them on a tray to dry out a little.

Preheat the oven to 180°C (350°F). Generously brush a 20 x 30 cm (8 x 12 inch) ovenproof dish with olive oil.

Finely grate the zest of the orange and squeeze the juice – you will need 125 ml (4 fl oz/½ cup) of juice.

Whisk together the eggs, sugar, olive oil, yoghurt, orange zest, orange juice and pomegranate juice in a bowl. When the mixture is smooth and slightly thickened, whisk in the baking powder.

Arrange a third of the filo ribbons in an even layer in the dish. Pour in a third of the egg mixture, then shake the dish a little and use a spatula to gently nudge the filo into the liquid. Repeat with the rest of the filo and egg mixture so that the filo is evenly spread in the dish and fully submerged. Bake for 30 minutes or until the pudding is set and the top is burnished.

Meanwhile, make the syrup. Combine the pomegranate juice, orange juice, marmalade and 100 ml (3½ fl oz) water in a saucepan. Stir over medium heat until the marmalade has melted. Add the sugar and stir until dissolved. Add the cinnamon stick and the orange skin and briskly simmer for 10 minutes. Set to one side.

As soon as you remove the cake from the oven, discard the orange skin and cinnamon stick from the syrup and pour the syrup over the cake. It might not be absorbed immediately, so add half now and the rest a little later if you like. Set aside for at least 1 hour so the cake can fully absorb all the syrupy juices.

Serve the cake cut into squares, with a dollop of Greek-style yoghurt.

These are elegant, tangy and delicious puddings – a sort of cross between a jelly and a mousse. They are perfect to make in advance: just bung the figs in the oven and assemble the plates when you're ready to eat them. This dish is loosely based on a Sicilian classic called *biancomangiare* (literally 'white dish'), although my version isn't quite so bridal white as I've added a fair bit of cinnamon. Some people get a little anxious cooking with gelatine but the sheets available these days make it a breeze – just soften them in cold water before adding to the warm (not boiling) liquid you want to set.

Almond-milk puddings with honey-roasted figs

Makes 4

12 g (¼ oz) gelatine sheets
125 ml (4 fl oz/½ cup)
    unsweetened almond milk
150 g (5½ oz) Greek-style
    yoghurt
120 g (4¼ oz) caster (superfine)
    sugar
2 teaspoons orange blossom
    water
½ teaspoon ground cinnamon
4 figs, halved lengthways
2 tablespoons honey
1 tablespoon olive oil
a pinch of salt
toasted flaked almonds,
    to serve

First you need to soften the gelatine. Simply place the sheets in a bowl, cover with cold water and set aside for about 5 minutes.

While this is happening, combine the almond milk, yoghurt, sugar, orange blossom water and cinnamon in a saucepan and whisk over medium heat until the sugar has dissolved and the cinnamon has amalgamated into the liquid. The mixture should be hot but not boiling. Pour into a heatproof bowl. Squeeze the excess water from the gelatine sheets, add them to the almond milk mixture and stir until completely dissolved.

Pour the mixture into four ramekins. Leave them to cool down for 10 minutes or so, then transfer to the fridge to set, about 4 hours.

About 50 minutes before you want to serve the puddings, preheat the oven to 180°C (350°F). Arrange the figs, skin side up, in a smallish ovenproof dish in a single layer, so they fit snugly. Whisk together the honey, olive oil and salt, and pour over the figs. Roast for about 20 minutes or until the figs are soft and the juices bubbling. Set aside for 20 minutes or so to cool down a little.

To serve, dip the ramekins in warm water, then run a knife around the edges to loosen and turn the puddings out onto serving plates. Sprinkle the almonds on top and divide the figs and the pan juices among the plates. Serve immediately.

Quinces are such a glorious fruit but quite contrary – they're hard as nails and bitter when raw, but fragrant, tender and golden pink when cooked. They can be difficult to find as the season is so short, so grab them when you can. This is a simple dessert, but the quinces come out of the oven so gorgeously perfumed that the result is absolutely divine.

Roast spiced quinces with rose-scented yoghurt

Serves 4

a squeeze of lemon juice
2 large quinces
1 cinnamon stick, broken in half
1 star anise
a pinch of saffron threads, chopped
2 bay leaves
4 small knobs of butter
1 tablespoon honey
3 tablespoons Muscat or other sweet wine

For the rose-scented yoghurt
100 g (3½ oz) Greek-style yoghurt
200 g (7 oz) ricotta cheese
¼ teaspoon rosewater, or to taste

Preheat the oven to 200°C (400°F).

Half-fill a mixing bowl with water and add the lemon juice. Using a very sharp knife and a great deal of care (quinces are incredibly hard), cut the quinces in half vertically along the core, and then cut each half into four wedges. Carefully remove the core and any fibrous bits, popping the wedges into the lemony water as you go. Leave the skins on – they will turn lovely and tender in the oven.

Spread a large double layer of foil on your work surface – it needs to be big enough to create a packet for the quinces. Drain the quinces well, place in the centre of the foil and bring up the sides to make an open packet. Add the cinnamon stick, star anise, saffron, bay leaves and butter, then drizzle over the honey and the wine. Tightly seal the packet and place on a baking tray. Roast for about 1 hour or until the quinces are very tender – the cooking time will depend upon the fruit.

While the quinces are roasting, prepare the rose-scented yoghurt. Whisk together the yoghurt, ricotta and rosewater, then cover and chill until needed.

To serve, divide the quince wedges among serving bowls, add a dollop of the yoghurt and drizzle with the cooking juices.

Every corner of the planet seems to have developed its own rice pudding and the Mediterranean is no exception, from cinnamon-spiked versions in Greece and Spain to fragrant bowlfuls scented with rosewater or orange blossom water in Morocco. I've flavoured mine with strong coffee and topped it with almonds encased in honey brittle – the flavours chime together a treat.

Espresso rice pudding with honey brittle almonds

Serves 4

200 g (7 oz) arborio rice

600 ml (21 fl oz) milk, plus extra if needed

200 ml (7 fl oz) strong espresso coffee

120 g (4¼ oz) caster (superfine) sugar

a splash of Pedro Ximenez sherry or other sweet sherry (optional)

2 strips orange zest

½ cinnamon stick

For the honey brittle almonds

olive oil, for brushing

40 g (1½ oz/¼ cup) almonds

3 tablespoons honey

1 teaspoon ground cinnamon

a pinch of salt

Get started on the almonds first. Line a dinner plate with a piece of foil lightly brushed with olive oil. Lightly toast the almonds in a dry frying pan over medium–high heat until they start to release their oils and turn golden. Shake the pan often so they don't burn. Pull the pan off the heat, stir together the honey, cinnamon and salt, and pour over the almonds. Shake the pan to coat the nuts in the sticky mixture – it will bubble up a bit – and return the pan to medium heat. Gently simmer the mixture for about 2 minutes, shaking the pan and stirring the almonds occasionally so they cook evenly and don't burn. Tip onto the foil-lined plate, spread the nuts out in a single layer, and put to one side to cool and harden.

Now, combine the rice, milk, espresso, sugar, sherry (if using), orange zest and cinnamon stick in a saucepan. Bring to a rollicking simmer, then reduce the heat and gently simmer, stirring now and then, for 25 minutes or until the rice is tender and the mixture is creamy. Add a splash more milk if the mixture looks too dry. You might need to adjust the heat during cooking – the mixture needs to stay at a relaxed simmer – and remove any skin that forms on the top.

Remove the orange zest and cinnamon stick and spoon the pudding into little glasses or bowls. Break or chop the almonds into pieces and scatter over the pudding. Serve immediately.

I love making this divine sorbet. Its glorious fuchsia colour fills me with happiness and the flavour combination is one I've never seen in the shops, which makes the very little effort involved in preparing it all the more worthwhile. Although there's no dairy involved, the texture is rich, smooth and creamy, and the fruity, berry flavour explodes in your mouth. It's a winner.

Pomegranate and strawberry sorbet

Makes about 1 litre (35 fl oz/ 4 cups)

4–5 pomegranates
120 g (4¼ oz) caster (superfine) sugar
30 ml (1 fl oz) lemon juice
400 g (14 oz/2⅔ cups) hulled strawberries

Halve and squeeze the pomegranates using a lemon squeezer. Tip the solids left in the squeezer into a strainer set over a bowl and press down with the back of a spoon to extract every last bit of juice. Measure out 400 ml (14 fl oz) of the juice, pour into a mixing bowl and add the sugar and lemon juice. Stir until the sugar has dissolved. Set to one side.

Pop the strawberries into a food processer and blitz until very smooth, stopping the machine now and then to scrape down the side of the bowl. Add the strawberry purée to the pomegranate juice and stir until well combined.

Now, freeze the mixture. If you are using an ice-cream maker, just follow the manufacturer's instructions. If not, pour the mixture into a lidded plastic container and pop it into the freezer for 1½ hours or until it is frozen just around the edges. Beat well using a hand whisk or electric beaters, then return to the freezer. Repeat this beating and freezing process every 1½ hours until the sorbet has frozen to a scooping consistency – if it hardens too much, just give it a final blitz in the food processor before serving for a creamier texture.

Apricots can be very disappointing – they promise so much with their blushing, downy skins but often prove as hard as turnips or woolly and flavourless. This dessert is the perfect way to use them. Don't be put off by the goat's milk yoghurt – the end result really doesn't taste of the farmyard, it just lends extra flavour and makes a great grown-up dessert. For the doubters, or those who really don't like goat's milk or cheese, full-fat Greek-style yoghurt will do nicely. You don't need to use an ice-cream maker for this (the freezer will be fine) but the results are creamier and lovelier if you do.

Goat's milk frozen yoghurt with roasted apricots and rosewater

Makes about 1 litre (35 fl oz/ 4 cups)

600 g (1 lb 5 oz) apricots
45 g (1½ oz) honey, or to taste
400 g (14 oz) goat's milk yoghurt
100 g (3½ oz) caster (superfine) sugar
¼ teaspoon rosewater
a pinch of salt

Start by roasting your apricots. Preheat the oven to 180°C (350°F). Halve and stone the apricots and place them in a roasting tin, cut side up. Squeeze a splodge of honey into the indent of each apricot half. Roast for 20 minutes, then flip the apricots and roast for a further 20 minutes or until the fruit is tender and the juices are bubbling and fragrant. Leave to cool completely, then blitz the fruit to a purée in a food processor or blender, adding extra honey to taste.

While the apricots are roasting, whisk together the yoghurt, sugar, rosewater and salt. Chill until the apricot purée has completely cooled. When this has happened, stir the apricot purée and yoghurt mixture together.

Now, freeze the mixture. If you are using an ice-cream maker, just follow the manufacturer's instructions. If not, pour the mixture into a lidded plastic container and place in the freezer for 1½ hours or so, or until frozen around the edges. Beat well using a hand whisk or electric beaters, then return to the freezer. Repeat the process every 1½ hours until frozen to a scooping consistency – if it hardens too much, just give it a blitz in the food processor before serving for a creamier texture.

Mini doughnuts drenched in honey. What more is there to say?

Fried dough bites with honey and lemon syrup

Makes about 60

250 g (9 oz/1⅔ cups) plain
   (all-purpose) flour
1 tablespoon cornflour
   (cornstarch)
1 tablespoon caster (superfine)
   sugar
1½ teaspoons ground allspice
½ teaspoon fine sea salt
2 tablespoons olive oil
2 tablespoons milk
vegetable oil, for frying
3 large eggs, lightly beaten
sesame seeds, for sprinkling

For the syrup

160 g (5½ oz) honey
2 tablespoons lemon juice
½ teaspoon ground cinnamon

First, make the syrup. Put the honey, lemon juice and cinnamon in a small saucepan set over low heat and stir to combine. Pull the pan half off the heat to keep warm while you make the batter.

In a mixing bowl, whisk together the plain flour, cornflour, sugar, allspice and sea salt. In a saucepan, mix together the olive oil, milk and 200 ml (7 fl oz) water, and heat until hot but not simmering. Tip the flour mixture into the olive oil and milk mixture in one go and stir continuously over medium heat until the mixture comes away from the side of the pan. Stir constantly for 1 minute more. Pull the pan off the heat and leave to cool for a couple of minutes.

While the batter is cooling, pour enough of the vegetable oil into a saucepan to come about 5 cm (2 inches) up the side and set over medium heat.

Gradually add the eggs to the cooled batter, beating well after each addition until smooth and completely combined (they will be tricky to amalgamate at first but keep stirring using lots of elbow grease).

Line a large plate with paper towel and pour half the syrup onto a separate large plate. Spoon the batter into a piping bag with a large star-shaped nozzle. When the oil reaches 150–160°C (300–315°F) on a sugar thermometer (or when a tiny piece of bread tossed into the oil turns brown in about 1 minute) squeeze the batter into the oil, snipping it into 3 cm (1¼ inch) strips with kitchen scissors. Fry gently for 5 minutes, turning the strips over in the oil so they are golden on all sides. If they turn brown too quickly, turn down the heat – you may have to keep adjusting the temperature. Scoop the cooked dough bites out of the oil with a slotted spoon. Briefly drain on the paper towel, then transfer to the honey syrup. Turn to coat, adding more syrup to the plate as you cook all the dough.

Leave the dough bites to soak up the syrup for at least 5 minutes. Scatter the sesame seeds over the dough bites before serving.

Index

A

alcohol 7, 8, 9
almonds
  Almond-milk puddings with honey-roasted figs 194
  Fig, almond and olive tapenade 47
  Witlof cups with almond tabouleh 40
apples and walnuts, Chargrilled witlof with sautéed 172
apricots and rosewater, Goat's milk frozen yoghurt with roasted 201
arancini with mozzarella, porcini and thyme, Spelt 60
Artichokes with broad beans, preserved lemon and almonds 148
asparagus
  Braised peas, broad beans and asparagus with tarragon, mint and shallots 160
  Charred spring onions, leeks and asparagus with romesco sauce 162
  Peach, shaved asparagus and lardo salad 78

B

Baked eggs with greens, avocado and yoghurt 34
Baked feta parcels with warm date syrup and walnuts 182
Baked mackerel with pine nut stuffing and roast cherry tomatoes 112
Baked orzo with squid 138
barley rusk salad with feta and caperberries, Mixed tomato and 73
Barley, haloumi and sorrel frittata 54
beans 135
  Cannellini bean and tahini soup with spiced chickpea croutons 93
  Gigantes beans and haloumi in spicy tomato sauce 136
  Lamb, orange and white bean stew 101
  Tuna with crispy gigantes beans and rocket salsa verde 116
beetroot with beetroot greens and balsamic, Roast 150

Beetroot, goat's yoghurt and watercress purée 45
Black lentils with sweet potato and tarragon–walnut dressing 143
Braised peas, broad beans and asparagus with tarragon, mint and shallots 160
bread
  Olive oil bread 19
  Pillowy pitta bread 20
  Tomato bread with mint, hazelnuts and jamon 33
broad beans
  Artichokes with broad beans, preserved lemon and almonds 148
  Braised peas, broad beans and asparagus with tarragon, mint and shallots 160
  Watercress and yoghurt soup with broad beans 90
broccolini, goat's curd and smashed pistachios, Penne with 129

C

cakes
  Chamomile and honey olive oil cake 188
  Fig, hazelnut and carob crumble cake 191
  Fig and lemon polenta squares 180
  Orange, thyme and semolina cake 183
  Pomegranate, orange and marmalade filo pudding cake 192
cancer 8, 9
Cannellini bean and tahini soup with spiced chickpea croutons 93
carob crumble cake, Fig, hazelnut and 191
carrots with carrot top dressing, Honeyed roasted 164
cereals 8
Chamomile and honey olive oil cake 188
Chargrilled witlof with sautéed apples and walnuts 172
Charred spring onions, leeks and asparagus with romesco sauce 162

Charred vegetables with preserved lemon dressing 152
cheese 6, 28–29
cheese pies with honey and za'atar, Crispy 30
Cheese, pea and spearmint rolls 64
cherries with basil and labna, Stewed 26
chicken with herbs and potatoes, Roast butterflied 104
chicken with ouzo, olives and charred lemons, Sticky 98
chickpeas with caramelised fennel and garlic yoghurt, Lentils, rice and 139
chickpeas, One-pan breakfast with Merguez sausages, eggs and 36
cholesterol 8
chorizo and potatoes, Warm baby octopus salad with 118
chronic disease 7, 9
Chunky fennel and radish tzatziki 42
Citrus and cinnamon compote 27
citrus salad with ricotta toasts, Olive, herb and 77
compote, Citrus and cinnamon 27
compote, Sticky plum and lavender 179
Confit shallots with herbs and garlic 153
Cooling tomato, almond and mint soup 82
crackers with whipped goat's cheese, Semolina and olive oil 53
Crispy cheese pies with honey and za'atar 30
cucumber salad with mint and rosewater syrup, Fruit and 12
Cured tuna with almonds and cucumber salsa 58

D

dairy 8, 28–29
dementia 7, 9
desserts 8
diabetes, type 2 7, 9
diet, Mediterranean 6–9
digestive problems 9
dough bites with honey and lemon syrup, Fried 202

E

eggplants
Eggplant and pistachio bites with spicy tomato sauce 59
Eggplants stuffed with rose veal, fennel and ricotta 103
Rigatoni with rich eggplant sauce 130
eggs 8
eggs and chickpeas, One-pan breakfast with Merguez sausages, 36
eggs with greens, avocado and yoghurt, Baked 34
Espresso rice pudding with honey brittle almonds 196
eye problems 9

F

Falling-apart, milk-roasted goat 102
Farfalle with creamy walnut pesto 128
farro, roasted vegetables and chestnuts, Warm salad of 140
fennel and radish tzatziki, Chunky 42
feta
Baked feta parcels with warm date syrup and walnuts 182
Figs, creamed feta and lavender honey on toast 22
Freekeh with feta, roast tomatoes and herbs 132
Tomato, feta and pistachio fritters 63
figs
Almond-milk puddings with honey-roasted figs 194
Fig, almond and olive tapenade 47
Fig, hazelnut and carob crumble cake 191
Fig and lemon polenta squares 180
Figs, creamed feta and lavender honey on toast 22
filo pudding cake, Pomegranate, orange and marmalade 192
fish 8, 9, 110–111
Baked mackerel with pine nut stuffing and roast cherry tomatoes 112
Cured tuna with almonds and cucumber salsa 58
Fisherman's stew with saffron aïoli 109
Roast whole red mullet with tomato, fennel and olive salad 120
Sea bass with saffron skordalia 119
Soused sardines on toast with pickled rhubarb salad 108
Tuna with crispy gigantes beans and rocket salsa verde 116
Fisherman's stew with saffron aïoli 109

Flatbreads with zucchini blossoms and ricotta 52
focaccia, Raspberry 176
Freekeh porridge with almonds and dates 21
Freekeh with feta, roast tomatoes and herbs 132
Fried dough bites with honey and lemon syrup 202
frittata, Barley, haloumi and sorrel 54
fritters, Tomato, feta and pistachio 63
frozen yoghurt with roasted apricots and rosewater, Goat's milk 201
fruit 6, 8, 9, 186–187
Fruit and cucumber salad with mint and rosewater syrup 12

G

galette with an almond crust, Peach and rosemary 184
garlic prawns with nduja, Sizzling 115
Garlic and yoghurt soup 86
Gigantes beans and haloumi in spicy tomato sauce 136
goat, Falling-apart, milk-roasted 102
Goat's milk frozen yoghurt with roasted apricots and rosewater 201
Goodness bowl with mint vinaigrette 74
grains 6, 134–135
Greek salad, Not-so-classic 69
Greek-style yoghurt and labna 24

H

haloumi and sorrel frittata, Barley, 54
haloumi in spicy tomato sauce, Gigantes beans and 136
hazelnut and carob crumble cake, Fig, 191
heart disease 7, 8, 9
honey and lemon syrup, Fried dough bites with 202
Honeyed roasted carrots with carrot top dressing 164
hummus with figs and walnuts, Pine nut 44

J

jam, Lemon thyme and tomato 50
Juicy pork chops with rosemary, juniper and braised fennel 106

K

Kale with garlicky lime yoghurt and almonds 168
Keys, Ancel 7
Koftas with sour cherries and tahini dressing 56

L

labna, Greek-style yoghurt and 24
labna, Stewed cherries with basil and 26
lamb
Koftas with sour cherries and tahini dressing 56
Lamb, orange and white bean stew 101
Yoghurt-marinated lamb with charred tomato relish in flatbread 96
leafy greens 6, 9, 156–157
leeks and asparagus with romesco sauce, Charred spring onions, 162
legumes 8
Lemon thyme and tomato jam 50
lemon-infused olive oil 157
Lentils, rice and chickpeas with caramelised fennel and garlic yoghurt 139
lentils with sweet potato and tarragon–walnut dressing, Black 143
lifestyle 7, 8
Lime and honey roasted pumpkin with mint yoghurt and pepitas 170

M

mackerel with pine nut stuffing and roast cherry tomatoes, Baked 112
Matchstick salad with nigella seeds 70
meat 8
Mediterranean diet 6–9
Mediterranean Diet Foundation 8
milk-roasted goat, Falling-apart, 102
Mixed tomato and barley rusk salad with feta and caperberries 73
mullet with tomato, fennel and olive salad, Roast whole red 120

N

Not-so-classic Greek salad 69
nuts 6, 8, 80–81

O

octopus salad with chorizo and potatoes, Warm baby 118
oily fish 9
olive oil 6, 7, 8, 48–49
Olive oil bread 19
olive oil cake, Chamomile and honey 188
Olive, herb and citrus salad with ricotta toasts 77
olives 8
omega-3 fats 9

One-pan breakfast with Merguez sausages, eggs and chickpeas 36
Orange, thyme and semolina cake 183
orzo with squid, Baked 138

P

pancakes with goat's curd and almonds, Peachy spelt 16
Parsley soup with walnut and lemon sprinkle 87
pasta
    Baked orzo with squid 138
    Farfalle with creamy walnut pesto 128
    Penne with broccolini, goat's curd and smashed pistachios 129
    Penne with zucchini, burrata and basil dressing 124
    Rigatoni with rich eggplant sauce 130
    Spaghetti with red witlof, bacon and garlic crumbs 127
peaches
    Peach and rosemary galette with an almond crust 184
    Peach, shaved asparagus and lardo salad 78
    Peachy spelt pancakes with goat's curd and almonds 16
peas
    Braised peas, broad beans and asparagus with tarragon, mint and shallots 160
    Cheese, pea and spearmint rolls 64
    Spelt risotto with pea and nettle purée 144
Penne with broccolini, goat's curd and smashed pistachios 129
Penne with zucchini, burrata and basil dressing 124
pies with honey and za'atar, Crispy cheese 30
pilaf with leeks and goat's butter, Wild rice 142
Pillowy pitta bread 20
Pine nut hummus with figs and walnuts 44
pistachio bites with spicy tomato sauce, Eggplant and 59
pitta bread, Pillowy 20
plum and lavender compote, Sticky 179
polenta squares, Fig and lemon 180
Pomegranate, orange and marmalade filo pudding cake 192
Pomegranate and strawberry sorbet 198
pork chops with rosemary, juniper and braised fennel, Juicy 106

porridge with almonds and dates, Freekeh 21
potato salad with samphire and almond butter dressing, Warm 167
Potatoes in paprika-spiked sauce 163
prawns with nduja, Sizzling garlic 115
pudding cake, Pomegranate, orange and marmalade filo 192
pudding with honey brittle almonds, Espresso rice 196
puddings with honey-roasted figs, Almond-milk 194
pulses 6, 134–135
pumpkin with mint yoghurt and pepitas, Lime and honey roasted 170
purée, Beetroot, goat's yoghurt and watercress 45

Q

quinces with rose-scented yoghurt, Roast spiced 195

R

radish tzatziki, Chunky fennel and 42
Raspberry focaccia 176
Retro tomatoes stuffed with spicy saffron rice and herbs 159
rheumatoid arthritis 9
rice
    Espresso rice pudding with honey brittle almonds 196
    Lentils, rice and chickpeas with caramelised fennel and garlic yoghurt 139
    Retro tomatoes stuffed with spicy saffron rice and herbs 159
ricotta, Flatbreads with zucchini blossoms and 52
ricotta pots with roast balsamic strawberries and pistachios, Whipped 15
Rigatoni with rich eggplant sauce 130
risotto with pea and nettle purée, Spelt 144
Roast beetroot with beetroot greens and balsamic 150
Roast butterflied chicken with herbs and potatoes 104
Roast spiced quinces with rose-scented yoghurt 195
Roast whole red mullet with tomato, fennel and olive salad 120
rolls, Cheese, pea and spearmint 64

S

salads
    Goodness bowl with mint vinaigrette 74
    Matchstick salad with nigella seeds 70
    Mixed tomato and barley rusk salad with feta and caperberries 73
    Not-so-classic Greek salad 69
    Olive, herb and citrus salad with ricotta toasts 77
    Peach, shaved asparagus and lardo salad 78
    Roast whole red mullet with tomato, fennel and olive salad 120
    Shaved zucchini with lemon herb dressing and walnuts 79
    Warm baby octopus salad with chorizo and potatoes 118
    Warm potato salad with samphire and almond butter dressing 167
    Warm salad of farro, roasted vegetables and chestnuts 140
    Wheat grain tabouleh with chervil and mint 72
sardines on toast with pickled rhubarb salad, Soused 108
sausages, eggs and chickpeas, One-pan breakfast with Merguez 36
Sea bass with saffron skordalia 119
seafood 6, 8, 110–111
    Baked orzo with squid 138
    Fisherman's stew with saffron aïoli 109
    Sizzling garlic prawns with nduja 115
    Warm baby octopus salad with chorizo and potatoes 118
    see also fish
seasonality 6, 8
seeds 8
Semolina and olive oil crackers with whipped goat's cheese 53
Seven Countries Study 7
shallots with herbs and garlic, Confit 153
Shaved zucchini with lemon herb dressing and walnuts 79
Sizzling garlic prawns with nduja 115
sorbet, Pomegranate and strawberry 198
soups
    Cannellini bean and tahini soup with spiced chickpea croutons 93
    Cooling tomato, almond and mint soup with walnut and lemon sprinkle 82
    Garlic and yoghurt soup with walnut and lemon sprinkle 86

Parsley soup with walnut and lemon sprinkle 87
Warming wheat grain and pomegranate seed soup 85
Watercress and yoghurt soup with broad beans 90
Yellow split pea soup with red onions and capers 88
Soused sardines on toast with pickled rhubarb salad 108
Spaghetti with red witlof, bacon and garlic crumbs 127
spelt
    Peachy spelt pancakes with goat's curd and almonds 16
    Spelt arancini with mozzarella, porcini and thyme 60
    Spelt risotto with pea and nettle purée 144
spring onions, leeks and asparagus with romesco sauce, Charred 162
squid, Baked orzo with 138
Stewed cherries with basil and labna 26
stews
    Fisherman's stew with saffron aïoli 109
    Lamb, orange and white bean stew 101
    Vibrant vegetable stew with capers, 154
Sticky chicken with ouzo, olives and charred lemons 98
Sticky plum and lavender compote 179
strawberries and pistachios, Whipped ricotta pots with roast balsamic 15
strawberry sorbet, Pomegranate and 198
stroke 9
sweet potato and tarragon–walnut dressing, Black lentils with 143

T
tabouleh with chervil and mint, Wheat grain 72
tabouleh, Witlof cups with almond 40
tapenade, Fig, almond and olive 47
tomatoes, 9
    Cooling tomato, almond and mint soup 82
    Freekeh with feta, roast tomatoes and herbs 132
    Lemon thyme and tomato jam 50
    Mixed tomato and barley rusk salad with feta and caperberries 73
    Retro tomatoes stuffed with spicy saffron rice and herbs 159
    Roast whole red mullet with tomato, fennel and olive salad 120

Tomato bread with mint, hazelnuts and jamon 33
Tomato, feta and pistachio fritters 63
tuna with almonds and cucumber salsa, Cured 58
Tuna with crispy gigantes beans and rocket salsa verde 116
type 2 diabetes 7, 9
tzatziki, Chunky fennel and radish 42

V
veal, fennel and ricotta, Eggplants stuffed with rose 103
vegetable stew with capers, Vibrant 154
vegetables 6, 8, 9, 156–157
vegetables with preserved lemon dressing, Charred 152
Vibrant vegetable stew with capers 154
vision problems 9

W
walnut pesto, Farfalle with creamy 128
Warm baby octopus salad with chorizo and potatoes 118
Warm potato salad with samphire and almond butter dressing 167
Warm salad of farro, roasted vegetables and chestnuts 140
Warming wheat grain and pomegranate seed soup 85
watercress purée, Beetroot, goat's yoghurt and 45
Watercress and yoghurt soup with broad beans 90
wheat grain and pomegranate seed soup, Warming 85
Wheat grain tabouleh with chervil and mint 72
Whipped ricotta pots with roast balsamic strawberries and pistachios 15
whole grains 6, 134–135
Wild rice pilaf with leeks and goat's butter 142
wine 8, 9

witlof
    Chargrilled witlof with sautéed apples and walnuts 172
    Spaghetti with red witlof, bacon and garlic crumbs 127
    Witlof cups with almond tabouleh 40

Y
Yellow split pea soup with red onions and capers 88
yoghurt 6, 28–29
    Garlic and yoghurt soup 86
    Goat's milk frozen yoghurt with roasted apricots and rosewater 201
    Greek-style yoghurt and labna 24
    Kale with garlicky lime yoghurt and almonds 168
    Watercress and yoghurt soup with broad beans 90
    Yoghurt-marinated lamb with charred tomato relish in flatbread 96

Z
zucchini
    Flatbreads with zucchini blossoms and ricotta 52
    Penne with zucchini, burrata and basil dressing 124
    Shaved zucchini with lemon herb dressing and walnuts 79

My heartfelt thanks go to Sue Hines, Corinne Roberts and Heather Holden-Brown for having faith, and the hugely talented team at Murdoch Books for creating such a stunning book. I'm thrilled to bits with the result.

The hugest hugs and gratitude go to my loyal outriders Adam, Ruby and Ben. Without your unstinting love and encouragement, tasting skills, dishwasher-unpacking ability and preparedness to run to the shops for me a gazillion times a day, this book would have been impossible. Mwah!

Published in 2016 by Murdoch Books,
an imprint of Allen & Unwin

Murdoch Books Australia
83 Alexander Street, Crows Nest NSW 2065
Phone: +61 (0)2 8425 0100
murdochbooks.com.au
info@murdochbooks.com.au

Murdoch Books UK
Ormond House, 26–27 Boswell Street,
London, WC1N 3JZ
Phone: +44 (0) 20 8785 5995
murdochbooks.co.uk
info@murdochbooks.co.uk

For Corporate Orders & Custom Publishing
contact our business development team at
salesenquiries@murdochbooks.com.au

Publisher: Corinne Roberts
Editorial Manager: Jane Price
Design Manager: Vivien Valk
Editor: Justine Harding
Design and Illustrations: Arielle Gamble
Photographer: Alan Benson
Food Preparation: Claire Pietersen; Claire Dickson-Smith
Production Manager: Alexandra Gonzalez

Text © Sue Quinn 2016
Design © Murdoch Books 2016
Photography © Alan Benson 2016

ISBN 978 1 74336 693 6 Australia
ISBN 978 1 74336 746 9 UK
A cataloguing-in-publication entry is available from the catalogue of the National Library of Australia at nla.gov.au
A catalogue record for this book is available from the British Library

Colour reproduction by Splitting Image Colour Studio Pty Ltd, Clayton, Victoria
Printed by 1010 Printing International, China

THANK YOU: The publisher would like to thank Earp Bros (earp.com.au) for the use of their beautiful tiles in the photography of this book.

MEASURES GUIDE: We have used 20 ml (4 teaspoon) tablespoon measures. If you are using a 15 ml (3 teaspoon) tablespoon add an extra teaspoon of the ingredient for each tablespoon specified.

IMPORTANT: Those who might be at risk from the effects of salmonella poisoning (the elderly, pregnant women, young children and those suffering from immune deficiency diseases) should consult their doctor with any concerns about eating raw eggs.

INTRODUCTION FOOTNOTES (pages 6-9)

1   http://sevencountriesstudy.com
2   www.unesco.org/culture
3   Primary prevention of cardiovascular disease with a Mediterranean diet. Estruch R, Ros E, Salas-Salvadó J, Covas M, Corella D, Arós F...Martínez-González MA (2013)
4   The effect of Mediterranean diet on the development of type 2 diabetes mellitus: a meta-analysis of 10 prospective studies and 136,846 participants. Koloverou E, Esposito K, Giugliano D, Panagiotakos D (2014)
5   Is the Mediterranean diet a feasible approach to preserving cognitive function and reducing risk of dementia for older adults in Western countries? New insights and future directions. Knight A, Bryan J, Murphy K (2015)
6   Adherence to a Mediterranean diet and survival in a Greek population. Trichopoulou A, Costacou T, Bamia C, Trichopoulos D (2003)

7   Definition of the Mediterranean diet: A literature review. Davis C, Bryan J, Hodgson J, Murphy K (2015) Mediterannean diet pyramid today. Science and cultural updates. Bach-Faig A, Berry EM, Lairon D, Reguant J, Trichopoulou A, Dernini S...and Serra-Majem L (2011)
8, 9 The European Food Information Council – Secrets of the Mediterranean Diet
10 Harvard School of Public Health
11 Tomatoes, tomato-based products, lycopene, and cancer: review of the epidemiologic literature. Giovannucci E (1999)
12 www.nhs.uk/livewell
13 Alcohol and cardiovascular health: the dose makes the poison... or the remedy. O'Keefe JH, Bhatti SK, Bajwa A, DiNicolantonio JJ, Lavie CJ (2014) www.hsph.harvard.edu/nutritionsource/alcohol-full-story/#possible_health_benefits